The Book of
ACTS

THE MORNINGSTAR VISION BIBLE

by Rick Joyner

The Book of Acts, The MorningStar Vision Bible
by Rick Joyner
Copyright © 2013
Trade Size Edition

Distributed by MorningStar Publications, Inc.,
a division of MorningStar Fellowship Church
375 Star Light Drive, Fort Mill, SC 29715
www.MorningStarMinistries.org
1-800-542-0278

International Standard Book Number— 978-1-60708-504-1; 1-60708-504-6

Cover Design: Kevin Lepp
Book Layout: Kevin Lepp

For a free catalog of MorningStar Resources,
please call 1-800-542-0278.

The Book of Acts
TABLE OF CONTENTS

PREFACE
THE MORNINGSTAR VISION BIBLE
BY RICK JOYNER

Next to His Son and the Holy Spirit, the Bible is God's greatest gift to mankind. What treasure on earth could be compared to one Word from God? There is good reason why the Bible is the bestselling book of all-time by such a wide margin. The importance of the Bible cannot be overstated. If Jesus, who is the Word, would take His stand on the written Word when challenged by the devil, how much more must we be established on that Word to take our stand and live our lives by it?

The most basic purpose of **The MorningStar Vision Bible** is accuracy and faithfulness to the intended meaning of the Author, the Holy Spirit. His written Word reveals the path to life, salvation, transformation, deliverance, and healing for every soul who would seek to know God. The universe is upheld by the Word of His power, so there is no stronger foundation that we could ever build our lives on other than His Word. Therefore, we have pursued this project with the utmost care in that what is presented here is His Word and not ours. We were very careful not to let anyone work on it that had an agenda other than a love for the truth and the deepest respect for the fact that we were handling this most precious treasure—God's own Word.

The primary accuracy of any translation is its adherence to the original text in the original languages the Bible was written in, Hebrew and Greek. However, there are problems when you try to translate from a language such as Greek into a language like English because Greek is so much more expressive than English. For example, there are several different Greek words with different meanings that are translated as one word "love" in our English version. The Greek words distinguish between such things as friendship love, erotic attraction, or unconditional love. When we just translate these as "love," then it may be generally true, but something basic in what the Author tried to convey is left out. As we mature in Christ by following the Spirit, these deeper, more specific meanings become important. Therefore, we have sought to include the nuances of the Greek language in this version.

A basic biblical guide we used for this work was Psalm 12:6: **"The words of the LORD are pure words; as silver tried in a furnace on the earth, refined seven times."** Every book we release of this version has been through a meticulous process to ensure faithfulness to the original intent at least seven times. Even so, we do not consider this yet to be a completed work. We are releasing these book by book in softcover to seek even further examination by those who read it. We are asking our readers to send us challenges for any word, phrase, or part that you think may not be accurate, along with your reasons. These will be received, considered, and researched with openness. If you have insights that you think should be added to the commentary, we will consider those as well.

You can email these or any comments that you have to bible@morningstarministries.org, or mail them to us at:

MorningStar Publications
375 Star Light Drive
Fort Mill, South Carolina 29715

Please include any credentials that you might have that would be relevant, but they are not necessary for this.

My personal credentials for compiling and editing such a work are first my love for the Bible and my respect for its integrity. I have been a Christian for more than forty years, and I have read the Bible through from cover-to-cover at least once a year. I do have an earned doctorate in theology from a good, accredited school, but have not used the title because I want my message received on the merits of its content, not by a title. Though I have been in pursuit of knowing the Lord and His Word for more than forty years, I still feel more comfortable thinking of myself as a student rather than an expert. If that bothers you I understand, but when handling the greatest truth the world has ever known, I feel we must be as humble and transparent as possible.

Most of those who have worked on this project with me have been students at MorningStar University. This is a unique school that has had students from ages sixteen to over eighty years old. Some have been remarkably skilled in languages, especially Hebrew and Greek. Some have been believers and students of the Word for a long time. Others were fairly new to the faith, but were strong and devoted to seeking and knowing the truth. These were the ones that I was especially interested in recruiting for this project because of the Lord's statement in Matthew 11:25:

> **At that time Jesus answered and said, "I thank You, Father, Lord of heaven and earth, that You have hidden these things from the wise and prudent and have revealed them to babes"** (NKJV).

Because **"God resists the proud, but gives grace to the humble" (see James 4:6; I Peter 5:5** NKJV), the humility of a relatively young believer can be more important for discerning truth than great knowledge and experience if these have caused us to become proud.

Also, as Peter stated concerning Paul's writings in II Peter 3:15-16:

> **Paul, according to the wisdom given him, wrote to you,**
>
> **as also in all his letters, speaking in them of these things, in which are some things hard to**

understand, which the untaught and unstable distort, as they do also the rest of the Scriptures, to their own destruction.

So the untaught can be prone to distort the truth if they are also unstable. This is why the relatively young believers that I sought to be a part of our team were not just stable but strong in the Lord and their resolve to know the truth.

Even so, not everyone who has great knowledge and experience has become so proud that it causes God to resist them. Those who have matured and yet remained humble and teachable are some of the greatest treasures we may have in the body of Christ. Such elders are certainly worthy of great honor and should be listened to and heeded. Nowhere in Scripture are we exhorted to honor the youth, but over and over we are commanded to honor the elders.

So it seems we have a paradox—the Lord reveals His ways to babes, but elders are the ones responsible for keeping His people on the path of life walking in His ways. This is not a contradiction. As with many of the paradoxes in Scripture, the tension between the extremes is intended to help keep us on the path of life by giving us boundaries. Pride in our experience and knowledge can cause us to stray from this path, as can our lack of knowledge if it is combined with instability. The vision and exuberance of youth are needed to keep the fire of passion for the Lord and His ways burning. This is why the Lord said that the wise brought forth from their treasures things both new and old (see Matthew 13:52).

For this reason, I sought the young in the faith who are also stable and displayed a discipline and devotion to obedience to the truth. I also sought the contributions of the experienced and learned who continued to have the humility to whom God gives His grace. As far as Greek and Hebrew scholars, I was more interested in those who are technically-minded, devoted to details, and who seemed to be free of doctrinal prejudices.

This is not to give the impression that all who worked on this project went over the entire Bible. I did have some who went over the entire New Testament, but most only worked on a single Book, and sometimes just a single issue. I may not have told many of the Greek and Hebrew experts that it was for this project when I inquired about a matter with them.

I realize that this is a unique way to develop a Bible version, but as we are told in I Corinthians 13:12 we "see in part" and **"know in part."** Therefore, we all need to put what we have together with what others have if we are going to have a complete picture. This version is the result of many years of labor by many people. Having been a publisher for many years, I know every editor or proofreader will tend to catch different things, and so it has been with this project. We also realize that as hard as we have worked on being as accurate as possible, we may have missed some things, and we will be genuinely appreciative of every one that is caught by our readers. Again, our goal is to have the most accurate English version of the Bible possible.

Even though accuracy and faithfulness to the original intent of the Holy Spirit were our most basic devotions, we also sought insights that could come from many other factors, such as the culture of the times in which the different Books of the Bible were written. Along with myself, many other contributors have spent countless hours of research examining words, phrases, the authors of the Books of the Bible, their times, and even the history of cities and places mentioned in it. Though the knowledge gained by this research did not affect the words in the text of the Bible, they sometimes gave a greater illumination and depth to their meaning that was profound. Sometimes they made obscure, hard to comprehend phrases come to life.

One of the obvious intents of the Author was to be able to communicate to any seeker of truth on the level they are on. For the most basic seeker, knowing such things as the nuances or more detailed meaning of the Greek or Hebrew words may not be important. As we mature, we will seek deeper understanding if we follow the Holy Spirit. We are told in I Corinthians 2:10, **"For to us God revealed them through the Spirit; for the Spirit searches all things, even the depths of God."** Therefore, those who follow the Spirit will not be shallow in their understanding of anything and will especially search to know the depths of the nature of God.

Our single greatest hope is that ***The MorningStar Vision Bible*** will reveal accurately the will and intent of the Lord, and compel all who read it to love Him more, which is the chief purpose of man. If we love Him more, we will then begin to love one another more. As we grow in love, we will also grow in our devotion to know Him even more, know His ways, and do the things that please Him. He deserves this from us more than ever could be expressed.

There is nothing greater than knowing Him. I am convinced that anything we learn about God will make us love Him more, which is our chief purpose and the one thing that will determine if we are successful human beings. This is also the only thing that can lead to the true peace and joy that is beyond anything this world could supply. There is no greater adventure that could be had in this life than the true Christian life. The Bible is the map to the greatest quest and the greatest adventure that we could ever experience.

INTRODUCTION
THE BOOK OF ACTS

The Book of Acts was written by Luke, a coworker of the Apostle Paul. Luke is also the author of the Gospel that bears his name. It was addressed to his friend Theophilus around the year 63 A.D. Its purpose was to record the work of the Holy Spirit in the spreading of the gospel by the apostles and to be a general history of the first-century church.

Acts begins where Luke's Gospel concludes, with the ascension of the Lord Jesus after His resurrection. Before He is taken up, the Lord promises His followers, "You will receive power when the Holy Spirit has come upon you; and you will be My witnesses both in Jerusalem, and in all of Judea and Samaria, and even to the remotest part of the earth" (Acts 1:8). The Book of Acts is the story of how this was accomplished by the first-century apostles. A main focus of the history written by Luke is how a new kind of apostle emerged, the missionary apostle, of whom Paul and Barnabas were a model and chosen to go to the Gentiles.

Following the Lord's ascension, His disciples returned to Jerusalem as instructed to wait for the promised Holy Spirit. The Spirit came on the Day of Pentecost, a Jewish holy day that symbolizes and prophesies the coming of the Holy Spirit. The one hundred and twenty disciples who received the Holy Spirit began to speak in different languages that were unknown to them personally, but were recognized by many of the spiritual pilgrims who had come to Jerusalem from all over the earth to celebrate the Day of Pentecost. This became a remarkable sign to them, as they heard the glory of God being declared in their native tongues. At the Tower of Babel, all men were scattered by different languages, and this was a sign that by the Holy Spirit all men would be gathered together again by the common language of the Word of God.

The Holy Spirit also turned the little band of fearful disciples into fearless witnesses of the resurrection of Jesus. The Apostle Peter, who had only recently denied the Lord, rose up to be one of the most important of all witnesses, preaching the gospel with great boldness and leading three thousand new souls to salvation on the church's birthday. As the outspoken leader of the disciples, Peter opened the door of the gospel to both the Jews and the Gentiles. From that time on, many others were continually added to the church by the witness of the apostles, while mighty signs and wonders from the Holy Spirit accompanied their witness. Thus the young church was born with power, and great courage was the hallmark of the first Christians.

The church was further strengthened as they devoted themselves to the apostles' teaching, to fellowship, to the breaking of bread with one another, and to fasting (see Acts 2:42). In this way, the new believers became disciples, students for life, seeking to learn from and emulate their Messiah. The wonders and miracles performed by the Holy Spirit kept the believers in a continual state of awe and wonder at the things that the Lord was doing. This would always be the true secret of their resolve—God Himself in their midst by the Holy Spirit, doing His works through them.

As a result of the teaching of the apostles and the power of the Holy Spirit, the young church grew stronger and gained favor with the people. However, the religious leaders of the Jews became jealous and threatened by the increasing influence of the apostles. This provoked the religious establishment to begin to persecute the apostles and any who professed Christ. Many were thrown into jail and tortured. Then Stephen, the first recorded Christian martyr, was stoned to death. Still, the believers maintained remarkable resolve and courage, even rejoicing that they had been considered worthy to be persecuted for the name of the Lord.

Chapter Eight introduces Saul of Tarsus, a Pharisee who after his conversion would become known as the Apostle Paul. This great apostle would give considerable definition to the purpose of the church and clarity to its message of the New Covenant. However, at the time of his conversion, he led a persecution against the church and its message. Many believers, both men and women, were dragged from their homes and taken to prison because of their belief in Jesus as the Messiah. On Saul's way to Damascus to arrest those who professed Christ there, the Lord Jesus Himself appeared to him in the form of a light so bright it blinded him. This resulted in Saul's repentance for his opposition to the gospel and a profound conversion to following Christ as his Lord and Savior.

Three days after Paul's conversion, a man named Ananias found Paul through the instructions he received in a vision. This otherwise inconspicuous believer was used to lay hands on one who would become possibly the greatest of the apostles. The humble Ananias was used to commission the great apostle and restore his sight. Paul would learn right away that the Lord wanted His people committed to not being respecters of persons because of class or status—any common person could be used to do the extraordinary, giving everyone value and purpose.

After Saul's conversion, he quickly became a powerful witness for the Lord. This caused his life to be threatened by the Jews, so he was sent far away to his home in Tarsus. After this, the young church enjoyed a time of peace. The next major event in the history of the church took place when the Apostle Peter took the gospel to a household of Gentiles. The Gentiles not only believed the gospel, but also received the gift of the Holy Spirit, just as the Jewish believers had.

When Peter went to the home of Gentiles, it resulted in a great controversy in the church—the ultimate clash between the religious traditions of the Jews and the gospel of grace, the basis of the New Covenant. The unity of the apostles and elders resolved this and the revelation of this purpose of taking the message of salvation to the Gentiles found in the Scriptures. This opened the door wide to the Gentiles to receive the gospel and take their place in New Covenant church life. From this point, the narrative is almost devoted exclusively to the spreading of the gospel among the Gentiles, resulting to a large extent from the extraordinary missionary ministry of the Apostle Paul.

The coming of the Gentiles to be full members of the church also brought about other controversies. Converts from among the sect of the Pharisees tried to persuade the Gentile believers that they had to be circumcised and keep the Law of Moses to be saved. A council of apostles and elders in Jerusalem dealt with this, which concluded that this burden should not be placed upon the Gentile converts. This freed the gospel from the shackles that some had tried to impose on it by compelling believers to keep the Law of Moses.

Through every trial, persecution, and controversy, the truth ultimately prevailed in the young church as it matured through its trials, becoming more refined in its methods. Even so, its basic message did not change—they preached Jesus and His resurrection from the dead. This message of hope and the power to live a victorious life continued its unprecedented spread throughout the world.

Luke's account of this formative period of the church ends with Paul in Rome as a prisoner awaiting his trial for preaching the gospel. Typical of Paul and Christians in general at the time, Paul kept right on preaching the gospel in Rome. This is but a snapshot of the history of the church—walking in great power, while remaining resolute and victorious in the face of great and continuous opposition. The message of life in the believers was so strong that they willingly faced death to share it. The world had never seen a force such as this before, but it has remained the nature of true believers throughout the church age, as it will to the end. The gospel, the Holy Spirit who ordains and anoints it, and the messengers who carry it, are an irresistible force and an immovable object in the earth. The truth will prevail, and that is the basic message of the Book of Acts.

NOTES

THE BOOK OF
ACTS
Acts 1

Jesus' Ascension

1   The former treatise I made, O Theophilus, concerning all that Jesus began both to do and to teach,

2   until the day in which He was received up into heaven, after He had given instructions through the Holy Spirit to the apostles whom He had chosen.

3   To these He also showed Himself alive after His passion by many proofs, appearing to them over a period of forty days, and teaching them concerning the kingdom of God.

4   As they were assembled together with Him, He charged them not to depart from Jerusalem, but to wait for the promise of the Father, which, He said, "You heard Me speak of.

5   "For John indeed baptized with water, but you will be baptized in the Holy Spirit not many days from now."

6   Therefore they asked Him, saying, "Lord, are You now going to restore the kingdom to Israel?"

7   He answered, "It is not for you to know the times or seasons that the Father has kept under His own authority.

8   "However, you will receive power when the Holy Spirit has come upon you. You will be My witnesses both in Jerusalem, and in all of Judea, Samaria, and even to the uttermost part of the earth."

9   When He had said these things, as they were watching, He was taken up, and a cloud received Him out of their sight.

10 While they were looking steadfastly into heaven as He went, two who appeared like men stood next to them in white apparel,

11 and said, "You men of Galilee, why do you stand looking up into the sky? This Jesus, who you saw received up into heaven, will come again in the same way that you have beheld Him go into heaven."

12 Then they returned to Jerusalem from the Mount of Olives, that is near to Jerusalem, only a Sabbath day's journey away.

13 When they had come in, they went up into the upper chamber where Peter, John, James, Andrew, Philip, Thomas, Bartholomew, Matthew, James the son of Alphaeus, Simon the Zealot, and Judas the son of James were all staying.

14 These were all in one accord, continuing steadfastly in prayer, along with the women, which included Mary the mother of Jesus, and His brothers.

Judas' Replacement

15 During these days Peter stood up in the middle of the brethren and said to the company of people gathered together, which numbered about one hundred and twenty, saying,

16 "Brethren, it was necessary for the Scripture to be fulfilled that the Holy Spirit spoke of by the mouth of David concerning Judas, who was a guide to those who arrested Jesus.

17 "For he was one of us, and received his part in this ministry."

18 Now this man obtained a field with the reward of his iniquity, and then plunging head first while hanging himself, he burst open so that his bowels gushed out.

19 This became known to all who dwell in Jerusalem, so that in their language that field is called Hakeldama, which means, the Field of Blood.

20 "For it is written in the book of Psalms, **'Let his habitation be made desolate, and let no man dwell in it. And let his office be taken by another.'**

21 "Therefore, of the men who have accompanied us the entire time that the Lord Jesus dwelt among us,

22 "beginning from the baptism of John to the day that He was received up from us, one of these must become a witness with us of His resurrection."

23 So they put forward two men, Joseph called Barsabbas, who was surnamed Justus, and Matthias.

24 Then they prayed, and said, "You, Lord, know the hearts of all men. Show which of these two is the one You have chosen,

25 "to take the place in this ministry and the apostleship from Judas who fell away that he might go to his own place."

26 So they drew lots for them; and the lot fell to Matthias; and he was numbered with the eleven apostles.

Jesus' Ascension

Acts 1:1-14: Here it is explained that Jesus went about to "do and to teach." He did the works first and then used them to teach from. All of His works were teachings with messages about the nature of God and men in order to bring them together again.

This first written history of the church starts on the most important foundation of Christianity—that Jesus rose from the dead and that He has ascended to sit at the right hand of the Father until the time has come to establish His kingdom on the earth. The understanding of how the first apostles took this message and built the church has been the basic guideline for all future ministry and missions.

One obvious question is: Why did Jesus leave the entire destiny of the church to disciples who had just denied Him and fled from Him during His greatest time of need? He was able to do this because His trust was not in these men but in the Holy Spirit who was about to be given to them. The Holy Spirit would transform this needy, fearful little band of humble followers into the most powerful force for truth the world had ever seen. For this reason, we should never judge what can be done by looking at those doing it, but by the Holy Spirit if He is with them. Never put limits on the Holy Spirit.

The great question of the apostles before His ascension was whether the Lord would at that time establish the kingdom. This has remained a dominant question to disciples in every generation, but as He instructed these, the timing of this must be left with the Father. We should focus on doing His work until the time.

Judas' Replacement

1:15-26: The choosing of Judas' replacement is given a lot of attention here even though we almost never hear of Matthias again. Some consider this to be an example of the methods and devices of church leaders until they were filled with the Holy Spirit when they came to depend on His voice and guidance. These also conclude that God's choice to re-place Judas was Saul of Tarsus, who was to become the great Apostle Paul. Perhaps. Certainly a good case could be made for this. Even so, the real issue is how the gospel took root and began to spread throughout the world, becoming the primary force shaping history. With the Holy Spirit, we can do the same for our own times.

NOTES

THE BOOK OF
ACTS
Acts 2

The Holy Spirit Comes

1 When the Day of Pentecost had come, they were all together in unity,

2 then suddenly there came from heaven a sound like a mighty wind, and it filled the whole house where they were staying.

3 Then there appeared to them tongues of fire that parted and sat upon each one of them,

4 and they were all filled with the Holy Spirit and began to speak with other tongues as the Spirit gave them utterance.

5 Now there were at that time dwelling in Jerusalem Jews and devout men from every nation under heaven.

6 So when this sound was heard, a multitude came together, and they were confounded because every man heard them speaking in his own language.

7 So they were all amazed and marveled, saying, "Look, are not all of these that speak Galileans?

8 "Then how do every one of us hear in our own native language?

9 "Parthians, Medes, Elamites, and the dwellers in Mesopotamia, in Judea, and Cappadocia in Pontus, and Asia,

10 "in Phrygia, and Pamphylia in Egypt, and the parts of Libya near Cyrene, and sojourners from Rome, both Jews and proselytes,

11 "Cretans and Arabians, we hear them speaking in our own tongues about the mighty works of God."

12 So they were all amazed, and perplexed, saying one to another, "What does this mean?"

13 Others were mocking, and said, "They are filled with new wine."

The First Gospel Preached by the Church

14 Peter, taking his stand with the eleven, raised his voice and said to them, "You men of Judea, and all of you that dwell in Jerusalem, let this be known to you, and listen closely to me.

15 "For these are not drunk as you suppose, seeing that it is only 9 o'clock in the morning.

16 "but this is that which was spoken through the prophet Joel:

17 'And it shall be in the last days,' says God, 'that I will pour out My Spirit upon the whole body, and your sons and your daughters will prophesy, your young men will see visions, and your old men will dream dreams.

18 'Yes, even upon My servants and on My handmaidens I will pour forth My Spirit in those days, and they will prophesy.

19 'I will show wonders in the heaven above, and signs on the earth beneath: Blood, fire, and vapor of smoke.

20 'The sun will be turned into darkness, and the moon into blood before the day of the Lord comes, that great and awesome day.

21 'Then it will be that whosoever will call upon the name of the Lord will be saved' (Joel 2:28-32).

22 "You men of Israel, hear these words! Jesus of Nazareth, a man proven to be approved by God by the mighty works that He did, signs and wonders that God did by Him in your midst, even as you all know.

23 "He was delivered up by you into the hands of lawless men to be crucified and killed, but this was predetermined by the counsel and foreknowledge of God.

24 "God raised Him up, having broken the cords of death, because it was not possible that He could be held by it.

25 **"For David said concerning Him, 'I beheld the Lord always before my face. For He is on my right hand that I should not be moved:**

26 **'Therefore my heart was glad, and my tongue rejoiced. Moreover my flesh also will dwell in hope;**

27 'because You will not leave my soul in Hades, neither will You give Your Holy One to see corruption.

28 'You made known to me the ways of life. You will make me full of gladness with Your presence' (Psalm 16:8-11).

29 "Brethren, I may say to you with confidence concerning the patriarch David that he both died and was buried, and his tomb is with us to this day.

30 "However, being a prophet, and knowing that God had sworn with an oath to him that from the fruit of his loins He would set One upon his throne,

31 "he foreseeing this spoke of the resurrection of the Christ, that neither was He left in Hades, nor did His flesh see corruption.

32 "This Jesus God did raise from the dead, a fact to which we all are witnesses.

33 "Being therefore exalted to the right hand of God, and having received from the Father the promise of the Holy Spirit, He has poured this forth, which is what you see and hear.

34 "For David did not ascend into the heavens, but he said himself, 'The Lord said to my Lord, "Sit at My right hand,

35 "until I make Your enemies a footstool for Your feet"' (Psalm 110:1).

36 "Let all the house of Israel therefore know for sure that God has made Him both Lord and Christ, this Jesus whom you crucified."

The Holy Spirit Promised to All Believers

37 Now when they heard this, they were pierced in their heart, and said to Peter and the rest of the apostles, "Brethren, what can we do?"

38 So Peter said to them, "Repent, and be baptized, every one of you in the name of Jesus Christ for the forgiveness of your sins, and you will receive the gift of the Holy Spirit.

39 "For this promise is to you and to your children and to all that are afar off, even as many as the Lord our God shall call to Himself."

40 With many other words he testified and exhorted them, saying, "Save yourselves from this crooked generation."

41 Then those who received his word were baptized, so that there were added to them about three thousand on that day.

The Church Matures

42 So they continued steadfastly in the apostles' teaching and fellowship, to the breaking of bread and prayer.

43 Fear came upon every soul, and many signs and wonders were done through the apostles.

44 So all that believed were in unity and had all things in common.

45 They sold their possessions and goods and distributed them to all according to the needs.

46 Day by day continuing steadfastly in unity in the temple and breaking bread at home, they took their food with gladness and singleness of heart,

47 praising God and having favor with all the people. So the Lord added to them daily those who were being saved.

The Holy Spirit Comes

Acts 2:1-13: The announcement that the Holy Spirit had come was the gift of tongues. By this gift those who had been baptized began worshiping and praising God in languages they did not know. Because it happened at a feast when Jews from around the world had gathered, these recognized the languages of their native lands and were understandably astonished by this, and gave their attention to Peter's explanation. As Paul would later write to the Corinthians "tongues are for a sign," the sign was that the church, which was built by God and not men, would be the antithesis to the Tower of Babel where the confusion of men's languages began. In this church, men of any language could understand and worship God in unity. This was a tower that would reach heaven because God would build it.

We also see here how some would marvel at the Holy Spirit, but others would mock. This continues to be true as those who do not marvel at the works of God will usually

mock them. There is no indifference when God is truly moving—we will either follow Him or oppose Him.

The First Gospel Preached by the Church

2:14-36: This is the first gospel message to be delivered by the empowered church, and beginnings are important. The message that brought salvation was the message of the atonement of the cross and resurrection of Jesus. When the Holy Spirit is poured out, signs, visions, dreams, and prophecy will occur. All other doctrines and messages that lead to God will start on this foundation.

The Holy Spirit Promised to All Believers

2:37-41: Those first to be converted by the preaching of the gospel were all promised the same gift of the Holy Spirit that the one hundred and twenty in the upper room had just received, and not only them, but as many as the Lord would call, which includes all who come to Him now.

The Church Matures

2:42-47: The first expression of church life was:

1) abiding in the apostles' teaching

2) fellowship

3) prayer

4) the fear of the Lord

5) signs and wonders

6) caring for one another

7) unity

8) the joy of the Lord

These remain the eight pillars of healthy New Testament church life.

NOTES

THE BOOK OF
ACTS

Acts 3

The Beautiful Gate Healing

1 Peter and John were going up into the temple at the hour of prayer, which was three o'clock in the afternoon.

2 There was a man who was lame from his mother's womb. This man was carried and laid daily at the gate of the temple that is called Beautiful so that he could ask alms of those who entered the temple.

3 When he saw Peter and John about to go into the temple, he asked them for money.

4 Peter, fixed his eyes upon him, and along with John, said, "Look at us."

5 So he turned his attention to them, expecting to receive something.

6 Then Peter said, "Silver and gold I do not have, but what I have I give to you—in the name of Jesus Christ of Nazareth, rise up and walk."

7 Then he took him by the right hand, raised him up, and immediately his feet and his anklebones were strengthened.

8 Leaping up, he stood, and began to walk. Then he entered the temple with them, walking, and leaping, and praising God.

9 All of the people saw him walking and praising God:

10 and they were staring at him, recognizing that he was the one who sat for alms at the Beautiful Gate of the temple, so they were filled with wonder and amazement at what could have happened to him.

11 As he clung to Peter and John, all the people ran together to them in the porch that is called Solomon's, wondering greatly at what had happened to him.

Peter's Second Gospel Message

12 When Peter saw it, he said to the people, "You men of Israel, why do you marvel at this man? Why gaze at us as if it was by our own power or righteousness that we made him walk?

13 "The God of Abraham, Isaac, and Jacob, the God of our fathers, has glorified His Servant, Jesus, whom you delivered up and denied before Pilate when he had determined to release Him.

14 "You rejected the Holy and Righteous One, and asked for a murderer to be granted to you in His place.

15 "So you killed the Prince of life, but God raised Him from the dead, a fact to which we are witnesses.

16 "It is by faith in His name this man has been healed, whom you behold and know. Yes, the faith that is through Jesus has given him his perfect health in the presence of you all.

17 "Now, brethren, I know that it was in ignorance that you did this, as your rulers did also.

18 "The things that God foreknew and revealed by the mouth of all the prophets, that His Christ should suffer, He has fulfilled.

19 "Repent therefore, and turn from your evil ways, that your sins may be forgiven, so that there may come seasons of refreshing from the presence of the Lord,

20 "and that He may send the Christ who has been appointed for you, even Jesus,

21 "whom heaven must receive until the time of the restoration of all things, about which God spoke by the mouth of His holy prophets from ancient times.

22 "As Moses indeed said, **'The Lord God will raise up for you a prophet like me from among your brethren. You shall listen to Him in all things He will speak to you.**

23 **'It shall be that every soul that will not listen to that prophet will be utterly destroyed from among the people'** **(Deuteronomy 18:15-19).**

24 "Yes, all the prophets from Samuel, and all of those who followed after him, as many as have spoken, also spoke of these days.

25 "You are the sons of the prophets, and of the covenant which God made with your fathers, saying to Abraham, **'And in your seed shall all the families of the earth be blessed' (Genesis 22:18).**

26 "Having raised up His servant, it was to you that God sent Him to bless you, to turn every one of you away from your iniquities."

The Beautiful Gate Healing

Acts 3-1-11: It was reported that Francis of Assisi was observing the great church structures in a city when his guide remarked about their splendor, saying, "We can no longer say that we do not have silver and gold." To this Francis replied, "And neither can we say 'rise up in the name of Jesus and walk.'" Money is the least valuable resource we have. It has value and is a resource, but compared to the spiritual authority we are called to have it is the least of our resources. Our worldly wealth will never be the basis of our witness to the world.

Peter's Second Gospel Message

3:12-26: The apostles immediately seized the opportunity that the miracle provided, getting the attention of the people to preach the gospel. This would lead to an even greater miracle—salvation. Miracles are called "signs" because they direct us to the Way. Just as a sign is not as important as the destination it points to, signs are not our final goal, but they are important.

NOTES

THE BOOK OF
ACTS
Acts 4

The Apostles Are Arrested

1 As they spoke to the people, the priests, the captain of the temple guard, and the Sadducees came upon them,

2 because they were extremely troubled as they taught the people and proclaimed through Jesus the resurrection from the dead.

3 So they arrested them and put them in prison until the next day because it was evening.

4 Even so, many of those who heard the word believed, and the number of the men had come to be about five thousand.

5 The next day the rulers, elders, and scribes were gathered together in Jerusalem,

6 and Annas the high priest was there, and Caiaphas, and John, and Alexander, and many others who were of high priestly decent.

Witness Before the Rulers

7 When they had set the apostles in their midst, they asked, "By what power, or in what name, have you done this?"

8 Then Peter, filled with the Holy Spirit, said to them, "You rulers of the people, and elders,

9 "if this day we are being examined concerning a good deed done to an impotent man, by what means this man was made whole,

10 "let it be known to you all, and to all the people of Israel, that in the name of Jesus Christ of Nazareth, whom you crucified, whom God raised from the dead, even by His name does this man stand here before you whole.

11 "He is the Stone that was rejected by you, the builders, that was made the Head of the corner.

12 "In no other name is there salvation. There is no other name under heaven that is given among men by which we can be saved."

13 When they beheld the boldness of Peter and John, and had perceived that they were unlearned and ignorant men, they marveled, and they recognized them as having been with Jesus.

14 Seeing the man that was healed standing with them, they could say nothing against it.

15 So when they had commanded them to go outside of the council, they conferred among themselves,

16 saying, "What should we do to these men? The fact that a notable miracle has been wrought through them is manifest to all who dwell in Jerusalem, and we cannot deny it.

17 "But so that it spreads no further among the people, let us threaten them not to speak to any man again in this name."

18 So they called them in, and charged them not to speak, nor teach in the name of Jesus.

19 However, Peter and John answered and said to them, "Whether it is right in the sight of God to obey you rather than to God, you be the judge.

20 "We cannot help but to speak about the things that we have seen and heard."

21 After they had further threatened them, they let them go, finding nothing to punish them for, because of the people who were all glorifying God for that which was done.

22 For the man was more than forty years old on whom this miracle of healing was wrought.

23 After being let go, the apostles came to their own company, and reported all that the chief priests and the elders had said to them.

24 When they heard it, they lifted up their voice to God together, and said, "O Lord, You made the heaven and the earth and the sea, and all that in them is,

25 "and by the Holy Spirit, through the mouth of our father David,

Your servant, You did say, 'Why do the Gentiles rage, and the peoples devise vain things?

26 "The kings of the earth set take their stand, and the rulers were gathered together against the Lord, and against His Anointed' (Psalm 2:1-2).

27 "For it is true that in this city, against Your holy Servant Jesus, whom You did anoint, both Herod and Pontius Pilate, with the Gentiles and the peoples of Israel, were united together,

28 "to do what Your hand, and Your council, foreordained to come to pass.

29 "Now, Lord, look upon their threats, and grant it to Your servants to speak Your word with boldness,

30 "while You stretch forth Your hand to heal, and to grant that signs and wonders may be done through the name of Your holy Servant Jesus."

31 After they had prayed, the place was shaken in which they were gathered together, and they were all filled with the Holy Spirit, and they spoke the word of God with boldness.

The Church Grows

32 The multitude of those who believed were of one heart and soul, and not one of them said that any of the things he possessed was his own, but they had all things in common.

33 With great power the apostles gave witness to the resurrection of the Lord Jesus, and great grace was upon them all.

34 Neither was there among them any that lacked, for those who owned lands or houses sold them and brought the price of the things that were sold,

35 and laid the money at the apostles' feet so that distribution was made to each, according to their needs.

36 Joseph, who was surnamed Barnabas by the apostles, which is interpreted, "Son of encouragement," a Levite, a man of Cyprus by race,

37 had a field, sold it, and brought the money and laid it at the apostles' feet.

The Apostles Are Arrested

Acts 4:1-6: Here we see the rulers were agitated by the apostles' message because they taught in the name of Jesus, and they taught the resurrection from the dead. These are the two most powerful truths that deliver men from the bondage of this world, and therefore those who are the rulers of this present world will be most threatened by these truths.

Witness Before the Rulers

4:7-31: This is the first great witness to civil leaders after the resurrection of Jesus, and the apostles stood boldly for the greatest and most important truths of the New Covenant— that Jesus is the only name in which there is salvation, and in His name there is power such as was demonstrated by the healed cripple who was standing with them.

Here the elders and leaders also perceived the source of the confidence and boldness of the apostles when they "recognized them as having been with Jesus." This is still the source of the boldness of those who stand for truth in face of all risk—they have been with Jesus.

Even after the apostles had testified with such courage, they asked the Lord for more boldness, and He sent the Holy Spirit and filled them again, even shaking the building they were in. It is always appropriate to ask for more courage to be a witness and to ask for a fresh filling of the Holy Spirit.

The Church Grows

4:32-37: There was such a unity and zeal for the Lord among the believers that they even sold or gave all of their possessions to be distributed among their fellow believers. Throughout church history, many have tried to duplicate this kind of fellowship and devotion, thinking that unity will come when we have all things in common like the church in Jerusalem. Almost always the reverse has been the result, with great divisions arising among the people. Why? What happened in Jerusalem with the people living with all things in common was never again demonstrated or taught in the New Testament. It was a unique situation in which it seems that the Lord was preparing His young church for the coming persecutions that would scatter them and then ultimately the destruction of Jerusalem. We must refrain from making anything a general doctrine or practice of the church that is unique in Scripture, unless there is a very clear leading from the Lord to do so.

NOTES

THE BOOK OF
ACTS
Acts 5

Ananias and Sapphira

1   At that time a certain man named Ananias, with Sapphira his wife, sold a possession and kept back part of the price.

2   With his wife also having knowledge of it, he brought a part of it, and laid it at the apostles' feet.

3   Then Peter said, "Ananias, why has Satan filled your heart to lie to the Holy Spirit, and to keep back part of the price of the land?

4   "While it remained, was it not your own? After it was sold, was it not under your control to do with it as you pleased? How is it that you have conceived this thing in your heart? You have not lied to men, but to God."

5   When Ananias heard these words he fell to the ground and died, so that great fear came upon all who heard this.

6   So the young men arose and wrapped his body, and they carried him out and buried him.

7   About three hours later his wife came in, not knowing what had happened.

8   So Peter inquired of her, "Tell me whether you sold the land for this amount?" She replied, "Yes, that is the amount."

9   Peter then said to her, "How is it that you have agreed together to test the Spirit of the Lord? Look, the feet of those who have buried your husband are at the door, and they will carry you out as well."

10 Then she fell down immediately at his feet and died. So the young men came in and found her dead, and they carried her out and buried her by her husband.

11 So great fear came upon the whole church, and upon all who heard these things.

Great Miracles Follow the Apostles

12 Many signs and wonders were wrought among the people at the hands of the apostles, and they were all in unity as they met in Solomon's porch.

13 However, the rest of the people would not come close to them, even though they held them in high esteem.

14 So more believers were continually being added to the Lord, multitudes of both men and women.

15 They even carried out the sick into the streets, and laid them on beds and couches, so that as Peter came by, at least his shadow might touch some of them and be healed.

16 Multitudes from the cities around Jerusalem also came together, bringing their sick folk and those who were oppressed with unclean spirits, and they were all healed.

The Second Arrest of the Apostles

17 Then the high priest rose up, and all that were with him of the sect of the Sadducees, and they were filled with jealousy,

18 so that they arrested the apostles, and put them in the public prison.

19 Then an angel of the Lord came at night and opened the prison doors, brought them out, and said,

20 "Go, stand and speak to the people in the temple the whole message of this Life."

21 So when they heard this, they entered into the temple about daybreak, and began teaching. When the high priest came, and those who were with him, they called the council together, and the entire senate of the house of Israel, and sent to the prison to have them brought.

22 When the officers that came did not find them in the prison, and they returned, saying,

23 "The prison we found shut securely and the guards standing at the doors, but when we had opened them, we did not find anyone inside."

24 Now when the captain of the temple guard and the chief priests heard these words, they were very perplexed concerning them, not knowing how this could have happened.

25 Then one came who said to them, "Behold, the men that you put in the prison are standing in the temple teaching the people."

26 So the captain and his officers went to bring them back, but did so carefully without any violence, because they feared the people, and thought that they might be stoned.

27 When they had brought them in, they set them before the council. So the high priest said to them,

28 "We charged you not to teach in this name, but you have filled Jerusalem with your teaching and intend to bring this man's blood upon us."

29 Peter and the apostles answered and said, "We must obey God rather than men.

30 "The God of our fathers raised up Jesus, whom you murdered, hanging Him on a tree,

31 "but God exalted Him to His right hand to be a Prince and a Savior, to give repentance to Israel, and the remission of sins.

32 "We are witnesses of these things, and so is the Holy Spirit, whom God has given to those who obey Him."

33 When the council heard this, they were pierced to the heart and intended to slay them.

Gamaliel's Counsel

34 Then one stood up in the council, a Pharisee named Gamaliel, a doctor of the Law, who was honored by all the people, commanded the apostles to be put outside for a little while.

35 Then he said to the council, "You men of Israel take heed to yourselves before touching these men. Think about what you are about to do.

36 "For before these days Theudas rose up, making himself out to be somebody, and about four hundred men joined themselves to him.

He was slain, and all who followed him were dispersed and came to nothing.

37 "After this man Judas of Galilee rose up in the days of the enrollment, and drew some of the people after him. He also perished, and all who followed him, were scattered abroad.

38 "Now I say to you, refrain from harming these men, and let them alone. For if this counsel, or this work, originated from men, it will be overthrown.

39 "But if it is of God, you will not be able to overthrow it, and you will be found even to be fighting against God."

40 So they all agreed with him, and when they had called the apostles back in, they had them beaten and charged them not to speak in the name of Jesus. Then they let them go.

41 The apostles therefore departed from the council rejoicing that they were counted worthy to suffer shame for the name of the Lord.

42 So every day in the temple and in homes, they did not cease to teach and to preach Jesus as the Christ.

Ananias and Sapphira

Acts 5:1-11: It is a dangerous thing to want to be identified with those who are giving their all for Christ, but secretly holding back part of the price or part of their hearts and commitment. This is the sin of lying to the Holy Spirit. This tragedy of Ananias and Sapphira is intended to warn all who do this that they are putting themselves in jeopardy. It is better to be honest and say we are holding back than to lie to the Holy Spirit. It is better still to hold nothing back from the Lord.

Great Miracles Follow the Apostles

5:12-16: The fear of the Lord that came upon the church after the episode with Ananias and Sapphira also resulted in great faith and great unity among believers. This resulted in great miracles and healings, not just for believers, but for all who lived around Jerusalem. As it says here, "all" who came seeking deliverance and healing received it. This is how the church age

started, and it is how it will end. The last-day church will walk in authority over all disease and all the power of the evil one.

The Second Arrest of the Apostles

5:17-33: The second arrest of the apostles resulted in the intervention of an angel to set them free. Even this remarkable miracle did not soften the hearts of the leaders whose motive we are told in verse 17 was jealousy. We are also told that it was because of envy that Jesus was crucified and likewise did many undeniable miracles that verified that He was sent by God. Jealousy is very powerful and is the basis for the hardest hearts.

Just as Jesus and the apostles walked in constant opposition from the jealous religious conservatives, this can be expected from all who walk in their footsteps. The spirit that ruled the Pharisees and Sadducees may be in different forms, but can still be found dominating many in the religious conservative community, and it will rise up in opposition to what God is doing.

Gamaliel's Counsel

5:34-42: Gamaliel's counsel may have sounded wise, and in one way it was, but it was also the way many approach the works of God, which keeps them from making a commitment to the work. That God was with the apostles was undeniable, and the greater wisdom was to acknowledge it and follow them. Gamaliel, the "wait and see" observer, is never heard from again in Scripture. The apostles went on to change the world.

After the apostles were beaten, they rejoiced that they were considered worthy to suffer shame for the name of the Lord. When we try to avoid shame by compromising, we are without basic understanding and a basic faith. Even the smallest honor with God is worth much more than any honor we can be given by men, and to be dishonored by men is often to be honored by God.

NOTES

THE BOOK OF
ACTS
Acts 6

Deacons Ordained

1   During these days, as the number of the disciples was multiplying, there arose a complaint by the Grecian Jews against the Hebrews, because their widows were being neglected in the daily distribution of food.

2   So the twelve called the multitude of the disciples together, and said, "It is not right for us to forsake the word of God to serve tables.

3   "Therefore, look for seven good men from among you, who are of good reputation, full of the Spirit and of wisdom, whom we may appoint over this duty.

4   "But we will continue steadfastly in prayer, and in the ministry of the word."

5   This pleased the whole multitude, so they chose Stephen, a man full of faith and the Holy Spirit, and Philip, Prochorus, Nicanor, Timon, Parmenas, and Nicholas a disciple from Antioch.

6   These were set before the apostles, and when they had prayed, they laid their hands upon them.

7   So the word of God increased, and the number of the disciples multiplied in Jerusalem exceedingly, and a great company of the priests were obedient to the faith.

The Witness of Stephen

8   Stephen was full of grace and power and wrought great signs and wonders among the people.

9   There arose some of the synagogue of the Libertines, as well as Cyrenians, Alexandrians, Cilicia, and Asia, who disputed with Stephen.

10 But they were not able to withstand the wisdom and the Spirit by which he spoke.

11 So they subverted men who said, "We have heard him speak blasphemous words against Moses, and against God."

12 And so they stirred up the people, as well as the elders and scribes, which came upon him, seized him, and brought him before the council.

13 Then they called up false witnesses who said, "This man does not cease to speak words against this holy place and the Law.

14 "We heard him say that this Jesus of Nazareth will destroy this place and change the customs which Moses delivered to us."

15 Then the whole council set with their eyes fixed on him, and they saw his face become like the face of an angel.

Deacons Ordained

Acts 6:1-7: The need of service to the widows resulted in the establishing of the great service ministry—the deacon. This ministry was considered so important that those appointed had to be of "good reputation, full of the Spirit and wisdom," because they were not just serving any people, but God's own household.

The Witness of Stephen

6:8-15: At least two of the deacons, Stephen and Philip, rose up with remarkable spiritual authority. Here it seems that the power of Stephen's witness and the miracles he performed may have eclipsed that of the apostles, evidenced by the focus of the persecution against him. Such maturing in the ministry of the Spirit should be the goal of all service ministries, because serving others is the foundation all other ministry is built on. Those who lay this foundation of being a servant can be trusted by God with greater power and authority.

NOTES

THE BOOK OF
ACTS
Acts 7

Stephen's Defense—that Jesus is the Christ

1 So the high priest asked, "Are these things true?"

2 Stephen replied, "Brethren and fathers, listen. The God of glory appeared to our father Abraham when he was in Mesopotamia before he dwelt in Haran,

3 "and said to him, **'Depart from your land, and from your relatives, and come to the land which I will show to you' (Genesis 12:1).**

4 "So he left the land of the Chaldeans and dwelt in Haran. From there, after his father died, God moved him to this land in which you now dwell.

5 "However, He gave him no inheritance in it, not even so much as to set his foot on, but He promised that He would give it to him as a possession, and to his decedents after him, even though at that time he had no child.

6 "Then God spoke about this, saying that his decedents would sojourn in a strange land, and that they would be brought into bondage, and oppressed for four hundred years.

7 **'The nation in which they will be in bondage I will judge,' God said, 'and after that they will come forth, and serve Me in this place' (Exodus 15:13).**

8 "He also gave Abraham the covenant of circumcision. Then he begat Isaac and circumcised him the eighth day. Then Isaac begat Jacob, and Jacob begat the twelve patriarchs."

Joseph as a Type of Christ

9 "The patriarchs, moved by jealousy against Joseph, sold him into Egypt, but God was with him,

10 "and delivered him out of all his afflictions, and gave him favor and wisdom before Pharaoh, the king of Egypt, who made him governor over Egypt and all of his house.

11 "Then a famine came over all of Egypt and Canaan. This brought a great desperation, and our fathers found no sustenance.

12 "When Jacob heard that there was grain in Egypt, he sent our fathers there the first time.

13 "The second time Joseph was made known to his brethren, and Joseph's relatives became known to Pharaoh.

14 "So Joseph sent for Jacob his father and all of his relatives, which were seventy-five in all.

15 "So Jacob went down into Egypt; and he died, along with our fathers,

16 "and they were carried over to Shechem, and laid in the tomb that Abraham bought for a price in silver from the sons of Hamor in Shechem.

17 "As the time of the promise that God had given to Abraham drew near, the people grew and multiplied in Egypt,

18 "until there arose another king over Egypt who did not know Joseph.

19 "The same dealt craftily with our people, and ill-treated our fathers so that they would cast out their babes and they would die."

Moses as a Type of Christ

20 "At this time Moses was born and was an exceedingly beautiful baby, and he was nourished three months in his father's house.

21 "When he was cast out, Pharaoh's daughter found him and had him provided for as her own son.

22 "Moses was instructed in all the wisdom of the Egyptians, and he was mighty in both words and deeds.

23 "When he was near forty years old, it was his desire to visit his brethren, the children of Israel.

24 "Seeing one of them being mistreated, he defended him and struck the Egyptian that was oppressing him.

25 "He supposed that his brethren would understand that God was by his hand giving them deliverance, but they did not understand this.

26 "The day following he appeared to two of them who were fighting with each other, and Moses tried to bring peace to them, saying, 'Sirs, you are brethren. Why do you fight with each other?'

27 "Then the one that was hurting his neighbor pushed him away, saying, 'Who made you a ruler and a judge over us?

28 'Would you kill me like you killed the Egyptian yesterday?'

29 "When Moses heard this statement he fled, and sojourned in the land of Midian, where he had two sons.

30 "When forty years had passed, an angel appeared to him in the wilderness of Mount Sinai, as a flame of fire in a bush.

31 "When Moses saw it, he marveled at the sight, and as he drew near to look, the voice of the Lord came to him, saying,

32 **'I am the God of your fathers, the God of Abraham, and of Isaac, and of Jacob.'** So Moses trembled and was afraid to look.

33 **"Then the Lord said to him, 'Loosen the shoes from your feet, for the place upon which you stand is holy ground.**

34 **'I have surely seen the affliction of my people that are in Egypt, and have heard their groaning, and I have come down to deliver them. Come, now I will send you to Egypt' (Exodus 3:1-10).**

35 "This Moses whom they rejected, saying, 'Who made you a ruler and a judge?' is the one God sent to be both a ruler and a deliverer by the hand of the angel that appeared to him in the bush.

36 "This man led them forth, having wrought signs and wonders in Egypt and in the Red Sea and in the wilderness for forty years.

37 "This is Moses who said to the children of Israel, 'God will raise up a prophet like me from among your brethren who will be similar to me.'

38 "This is he that was in the congregation in the wilderness with the angel that spoke to him at Mount Sinai, and with our fathers, who received living oracles to give to us,

39 "and to whom our fathers would not be obedient, but pushed him away from them, and turned back in their hearts to Egypt,

40 "saying to Aaron, 'Make us gods that shall go before us. As for this Moses, who led us out of the land of Egypt, we do not know what has happened to him.'

41 "So they made a calf at that time, and made sacrifices to the idol, and rejoiced in the works of their own hands.

42 "So God turned and gave them up to serve the host of heaven; as it is written in the book of the prophets, **'Did you offer to me slain beasts and sacrifices for forty years in the wilderness, O house of Israel? (Jeremiah 19:13).**

43 **'You took up the tabernacle of Moloch, and the star of the god Rephan, the figures which you made to worship them. So I will carry you away beyond Babylon' (Amos 5:25-27).**

44 "Our fathers had the tabernacle of the testimony in the wilderness, even as the one who appointed Moses spoke to him that he should make it according to the pattern that he had seen."

David and Solomon as Types of Christ

45 "This is the tabernacle that our fathers brought into the land with Joshua when they took possession of the nations that God thrust out before the face of our fathers, until the days of David,

46 "who found favor in the sight of God, and asked to build a habitation for the God of Jacob.

47 "Yet Solomon built Him a house,

48 "even though the Most High does not dwell in houses made with hands, even as the prophet said,

49 **'Heaven is My throne, and the earth the footstool of My feet. What kind of house will you build Me? Or what is the place of My rest?'** says the Lord.

50 **'Did not my hand make all these things?'" (Isaiah 66:1-2).**

Stephen Rebukes the Council

51 "You stiff-necked and uncircumcised in heart and ears, you always resist the Holy Spirit just as your fathers did.

52 "Which of the prophets did your fathers not persecute? They killed those who prophesied the coming of the Righteous One, whose betrayers and murderers you have now become.

53 "You received the law as if it was ordained by angels, but did not keep it."

54 Now when they heard these things, they were cut to the heart, and they gnashed their teeth at him.

55 He being full of the Holy Spirit looked up steadfastly into heaven and saw the glory of God and Jesus standing on the right hand of God,

56 and said, "Look! I see the heavens opened, and the Son of Man standing at the right hand of God!"

Stephen Martyred

57 Then they cried out with a loud voice, and stopped their ears, and rushed upon him with one accord,

58 dragging him outside of the city, and stoned him, laying their garments at the feet of a young man named Saul who witnessed it.

59 As they stoned Stephen, he called upon the Lord, saying, "Lord Jesus, receive my spirit."

60 Then he kneeled down, and cried with a loud voice, "Lord, do not lay this sin to their charge." When he had said this, he fell asleep.

Stephen's Defense—that Jesus is the Christ

Acts 7:1-8: Stephen begins his defense by recounting the basic history of Israel, especially focusing on all whose lives were a type of their Messiah. In this history, it is apparent how Jesus fulfilled the prophecies.

Joseph as a Type of Christ

7:9-19: Here it is explained how Joseph was a type of Christ and how his life mirrored that of Jesus by being rejected by his brothers, but this was for their salvation, just as it was for Jesus.

Moses as a Type of Christ

7:20-44: Here Stephen establishes Moses as a type of Christ, who like Jesus was rejected by his brethren the first time he came to them as a deliverer. However, the second time Moses came to them it was with great power and authority, which Jesus will likewise do.

David and Solomon as Types of Christ

7:45-50: Here Stephen mentions two more prominent types of Christ, David and Solomon. This also brings in the important factor of how their purpose was to build God a permanent habitation so the that He could dwell among His people, which Jesus is likewise doing with the church.

Stephen Rebukes the Council

7:51-56: Here Stephen likens the council to all of the previous elders of Israel who rejected God's messengers and types of Christ, but the present ones have actually rejected Christ. This enrages the council, but when Stephen sees Christ in this vision, his tone changes to one of conciliation and forgiveness.

Stephen Martyred

7:57-60: The young Saul witnesses the first Christian martyrdom, an event that after his conversion would likely be a main drive to his extraordinary motivation to preach the gospel of the kingdom.

NOTES

THE BOOK OF
ACTS
Acts 8

Saul Persecutes the Church

1 Saul consented to Stephen's death. On that same day there arose a great persecution against the church that was in Jerusalem, so that the believers were all scattered abroad throughout the regions of Judea and Samaria, except for the apostles who remained in Jerusalem.

2 The devout men buried Stephen, and made great lamentation over him.

3 So Saul laid waste to the church, entering into every house, and dragging men and women to prison.

4 However, those who were scattered abroad went about preaching the word.

Philip Stirs Samaria

5 Philip went down to the city of Samaria and proclaimed Christ to them.

6 The multitudes gave heed with one accord to the things that were spoken by Philip when they saw and heard the signs that he performed.

7 Many unclean spirits came out of those who had them, and they were crying out with a loud voice. Others that were afflicted with the palsy and who were lame were healed.

8 So there was great joy in that city.

Simon the Sorcerer

9 There was a certain man, Simon by name, who before this used sorcery to amaze the people of Samaria, making himself out to be someone great.

10 They were all giving heed to him from the least to the greatest, saying, "This man has great power from God."

11 They gave heed to him because for a long time he had amazed them with his sorceries,

12 but when they believed Philip preaching good news about the kingdom of God in the name of Jesus Christ, they were baptized, both men and women.

13 Simon also believed, and after being baptized, he continued with Philip, and seeing the signs and great miracles wrought, he was amazed.

Apostles Are Sent to Samaria

14 Now when the apostles who were in Jerusalem heard that Samaria had received the word of God, they sent Peter and John to them.

15 When they had arrived, they prayed for the new believers to receive the Holy Spirit,

16 because as yet He had not fallen upon any one, but they had only been baptized into the name of the Lord Jesus.

17 When they laid their hands on the believers they received the Holy Spirit.

Simon's Sin

18 Now when Simon saw that it was through the laying on of the apostles' hands that the Holy Spirit was given, he offered them money,

19 saying, "Give me this power, so that on whomever I lay my hands they may receive the Holy Spirit."

20 Peter said to him, "May your silver perish with you, because you have thought that you could obtain the gift of God with money.

21 "You have no part or lot in this matter because your heart is not right before God.

22 "Therefore, repent of this wickedness, and pray to the Lord so that perhaps the intent of your heart may be forgiven you.

23 "For I see that you are in the gall of bitterness and in the bond of iniquity."

24 Simon answered and said, "You pray for me to the Lord that none of the things which you have spoken will come upon me."

25 Therefore, when they had testified and spoken the word of the Lord, as they returned to Jerusalem they preached the gospel to many villages of the Samaritans.

The Ethiopian Eunuch

26 Then an angel of the Lord spoke to Philip, saying, "Arise, and go toward the south, to the way that goes down from Jerusalem to Gaza, which is desert."

27 So he arose and went, and a man of Ethiopia, a eunuch of great authority under Candace, queen of the Ethiopians, who was over all her treasure, and had come to Jerusalem to worship, and was returning.

28 As he sat in his chariot, he was reading the prophet Isaiah.

29 The Spirit said to Philip, **"Go near and join yourself to this chariot."**

30 Philip ran to him, and heard him reading Isaiah the prophet, and said, "Do you understand what you are reading?"

31 He replied, "How can I, unless someone guides me?" So he asked Philip to come up and sit with him.

32 Now the passage of the Scripture that he was reading was, **"He was led as a sheep to the slaughter. As a lamb is before his shearer is dumb, so he did not open His mouth.**

33 **"In his humiliation He was taken away for judgment. Who will declare this from His generation? For his life is taken from the earth" (Isaiah 53:7-8).**

34 So the eunuch asked Philip, "Please tell me, about who does the prophet says this? Is it himself or someone else?"

35 Then Philip began from this Scripture, and preached Jesus to him.

36 As they went on the way, they came to some water, and the eunuch said, "Look, water! What hinders me from being baptized?"

37 Philip said, "If you believe with all of your heart, you may be baptized." He answered and said, "I believe that Jesus Christ is the Son of God."

38 So he commanded the chariot to stop, and they both went down into the water, and Philip baptized him.

Philip Is Translated

39 When they came up out of the water, the Spirit of the Lord caught Philip away, so that he disappeared, and the eunuch did not see him anymore. So he went on his way rejoicing.

40 Philip found himself at Azotus, and passing through he preached the gospel to all the cities, until he came to Caesarea.

Saul Persecutes the Church

Acts 8:1-4: Revivals have been sparked by just one person who is in pursuit of God in an extraordinary way, and they have been ignited by persecutions, such as the case here. As we see here and throughout history, it is a basic characteristic of the church that whenever it is persecuted, it expands and grows. Persecution purifies, empowers, and emboldens those who love the truth more than their own lives.

Philip Stirs Samaria

8:5-8: Samaria was populated by those who had a mixture of other nations in their Jewish heritage, and also had a mixture in their spiritual beliefs. As we see here, and in the case of Jesus speaking to the woman at the well, the Samaritans were the most responsive of all to the gospel. In each case, the entire city responded. For this reason, we should never give up on those who may have a mixture in their doctrine, but have a love and zeal for God.

Simon the Sorcerer

8:9-13: The miracles of God will always eclipse the power of the enemy. As we see here, sorceries are almost always used to amaze people and exalt the sorcerer. However, the power of God does not just amaze people, but heals them and sets them free, and then the people exalt Jesus.

Apostles are Sent to Samaria

8:14-17: The first thing that the apostles did to establish the new believers in the faith was to pray for them to receive the baptism in the Holy Spirit. This passage is also evidence that the baptism is not automatically given to a new believer, even though they are water baptized in the name of Jesus, but we must pray for this experience separately.

Simon's Sin

8:18-25: Simon's sin was to belittle the gift of God, thinking that it could be purchased with money and dishonoring God by implying that His gifts could be bought. All of the gifts and grace of God were purchased by the blood of the Son of God, and no amount of earthly treasure could ever compare to that. Simon the sorcerer also had an evil motive in seeking the gift so that he could further his on prominence among the people. One of the most profane things we can ever do is seek the gifts of God in order to promote ourselves rather than to promote the Son of God.

The Ethiopian Eunuch

8:26-38: How many could obey the Lord to leave a revival that was impacting an entire city to go minister to just one man? Why would the Lord have Philip do this? A single soul is infinitely valuable to Him, but there seems to have been much more to this that was only revealed centuries later when explorers went to Ethiopia and found it to be a Christian nation. We do not know whether one person will be more fruitful for the gospel than an entire city that is baptized, so our devotion always must be to simply obey the Holy Spirit.

Philip Is Translated

8:39-40: Here we see that Philip was translated by the Holy Spirit to another place. This experience has happened to others as well, even in our own times. Philip went on preaching the gospel. Such was the devotion of believers in the first century—wherever you are, however you get there, preach the gospel.

NOTES

The Book of
ACTS
Acts 9

Saul's Conversion

1 Saul continued to make threats and seek to destroy the disciples of the Lord, and so he went to the high priest

2 and asked for letters from him to the synagogues in Damascus, so that if he found any that were of The Way there, whether men or women, he might bring them bound to Jerusalem.

3 As he journeyed and came near to Damascus, suddenly a light out of heaven shone all around him, so he fell to the ground.

4 Then he heard a voice saying to him, "Saul! Saul! Why are you persecuting Me?"

5 He replied, "Who are You, Lord?" He said, "I am Jesus whom you are persecuting.

6 "Rise, and enter into the city, and it will be told to you what you must do."

7 The men that journeyed with him stood speechless, hearing the voice, but not seeing anyone.

8 Saul arose from the ground, and when he opened his eyes he could not see. So they led him by the hand and brought him to Damascus.

9 He went three days without sight and did not eat nor drink.

10 Now there was a certain disciple in Damascus, named Ananias, and the Lord said to him in a vision, "Ananias." He answered, "Here I am, Lord."

11 Then the Lord said to him, "Arise, and go to the street that is called Straight, and inquire in the house of Judas for one named Saul, a man from Tarsus, who is there praying.

12 "He has seen a man named Ananias coming and laying his hands on him, so that he can receive his sight."

13 Ananias answered, "Lord, I have heard from many about this man, how much evil he did to Your saints in Jerusalem,

14 "and here he was given authority from the chief priests to bind all that call upon Your name."

15 The Lord said to him, "Go your way because he is a chosen vessel of Mine to bear My name before the Gentiles and kings and the children of Israel,

16 "and I will show him how many things he must suffer for My name's sake."

17 So Ananias departed, and entered into the house, and laying his hands on him said, "Brother Saul, the Lord Jesus, Who appeared to you on the way in which you came, has sent me so that you may receive your sight, and be filled with the Holy Spirit."

18 Immediately there were like scales that fell from his eyes, and he received his sight, and he arose and was baptized.

19 Then he took food and was strengthened. So he then stayed with the disciples that were in Damascus for several days.

Saul Preaches Christ

20 Immediately Saul proclaimed Jesus in the synagogues, declaring that He is indeed the Son of God.

21 All who heard him were amazed and said, "Is this not the one who in Jerusalem made havoc for those who called on this name? Did he not come here with the intent of bringing them bound before the chief priests?"

22 Saul increased even more in power and confounded the Jews that dwelt at Damascus, proving that Jesus is the Christ.

23 After many days had passed, the Jews took counsel together to kill him, but their plot became known to Saul.

24 Because they were watching the gates day and night so that they might kill him,

25 his disciples took him by night, and let him down through the wall, lowering him in a basket.

26 When he had come to Jerusalem, he tried to join the disciples, but they were all afraid of him, not believing that he was a disciple.

27 However, Barnabas took him and brought him to the apostles and declared to them how he had seen the Lord on the way, and that He had spoken to him, and how in Damascus he had preached boldly in the name of Jesus.

28 So he was with them going in and going out of Jerusalem, preaching boldly in the name of the Lord.

29 As he spoke and disputed with the Grecian Jews, they too sought to kill him.

30 So when the brethren learned of it, they brought him down to Caesarea and sent him to Tarsus.

31 So the church throughout all Judea and Galilee and Samaria had peace and was multiplying, being built up and walking in the fear of the Lord and in the comfort of the Holy Spirit.

Extraordinary Miracles Wrought Through Peter

32 So it came to pass as Peter went throughout all of those parts, he came down to the saints that dwelt at Lydda.

33 There he found a certain man named Aeneas, who was kept in his bed for eight years because he was palsied.

34 Peter said to him, "Aeneas, Jesus Christ heals you. Arise and make your bed." Immediately he arose.

35 All that dwelt at Lydda and in Sharon saw him and turned to the Lord.

36 Now there was at Joppa a certain disciple named Tabitha, which by interpretation is called Tabitha (Dorcas). This woman was full of good works and gave many alms.

37 At that time she fell sick and died. When they had washed her, they laid her in an upper chamber.

38 As Lydda was near to Joppa, the disciples, hearing that Peter was there, sent two men to entreat him, "Do not delay to come to us."

39 So Peter arose and went with them. When he had come, they brought him into the upper chamber where all the widows stood by him weeping, and showing the coats and garments which Dorcas made while she was with them.

40 Then Peter sent them all out, and kneeled down and prayed, and turning to the body, he said, "Tabitha, arise." She opened her eyes, and when she saw Peter she sat up.

41 He gave her his hand, raised her up, and calling the saints and widows, he presented her alive.

42 So it became known throughout all Joppa, and many believed in the Lord.

43 So Peter stayed many days in Joppa with Simon, a tanner.

Saul's Conversion

Acts 9:1-19: The conversion of Saul is possibly the most dramatic conversion in church history and certainly one of the most consequential. The man who was the greatest enemy of the faith was instantly transformed and became one of its greatest witnesses for Christ. This is the power of conversion and what it means to be born again.

Because Saul's worldview that had been based on the Law had brought him into such direct conflict with the truth, when converted, he grasped the depths of the New Covenant like few ever have and became possibly its greatest champion. Paul is still most likely the greatest apostle to ever live. Should this not give us hope for even the most hardened against the Lord? We should never give up on anyone. Through Christ, even our greatest enemies can become our best friends.

Saul Preaches Christ

9:20-31: Saul does not waste any time preaching the truth that had been revealed to him—that Jesus is the Son of God. As we also see in verse 25, he had already begun making disciples. This is the nature of true Christian leadership—the bold proclamation of the gospel and making disciples and fulfilling The Great Commission.

Extraordinary Miracles Wrought Through Peter

9:32-43: It is apparent that the mode of operation for the apostles was to fulfill the command of the Lord to heal the sick, raise the dead, and cast out demons everywhere they went. This caused the gospel of Christ to be built upon the foundation that God loved people, wanted to do good for them, and would if they believed in Him. This has not changed.

NOTES

THE BOOK OF
ACTS
Acts 10

The Vision of Cornelius

1   Now there was a certain man in Caesarea named Cornelius who
    was a centurion with the Italian cohort.

2   He was a devout man who feared God along with his whole house.
    He gave many alms to the people and prayed to God continually.

3   At the time of the evening offering he saw in an open vision an
    angel of God coming to him, and saying, "Cornelius."

4   As he was looking directly at him, and being frightened, he replied,
    "What is it, Lord?" He said to him, "Your prayers and your alms
    have gone up as a memorial before God.

5   "Now send men to Joppa to find and bring here one called Simon,
    who is surnamed Peter.

6   "He is lodging with Simon, a tanner, whose house is by the sea."

7   When the angel that spoke to him departed, he called two of his
    household servants, and a devout soldier of those who were in
    constant attendance with him,

8   and after he rehearsed all of these things to them, he sent them
    to Joppa.

Peter Goes to the Gentiles

9   Now on the next day, as they were on their journey, and drew near
    to the city, Peter went up on the housetop to pray at about noon.

10 Then he became hungry and desired to eat. While they prepared
    food for him, he fell into a trance.

11 He saw the heavens opened and a certain vessel descending like a great sheet being let down by its four corners to the earth.

12 In it were all manner of four-footed beasts and creeping things of the earth and birds of the sky.

13 Then a voice came to him, saying, "Arise Peter! Kill and eat."

14 Peter replied, "No Lord. I have never eaten anything that is common or unclean."

15 The voice came to him a second time, saying, "What God has cleansed, do not call unclean."

16 This was done three times, and then the vessel was received up into heaven.

17 Now while Peter was very perplexed about what the vision might mean, the men who were sent by Cornelius, having made inquiry for Simon's house, stood outside the gate,

18 and called and asked whether Simon, who was surnamed Peter, was lodging there.

19 While Peter pondered the vision, the Spirit said to him, "Behold, three men are seeking you.

20 "Arise, go down, and go with them without doubting, because I have sent them."

21 So Peter went down to the men, and said, "I am the one you are seeking. Why have you come?"

22 They said, "Cornelius, a centurion, and a righteous man who fears God, and who has a good reputation with the whole nation of the Jews, was told by God through a holy angel to send for you at this house, and to hear a message from you."

23 So he called them in, and they lodged there that night. On the next day Peter arose and went with them, and some of the brethren from Joppa accompanied him.

24 On the next day they entered Caesarea, and Cornelius was waiting for them, having called together his kinsmen and his close friends.

25 When Peter entered, Cornelius met him and fell down at his feet and worshiped him.

26 Peter raised him up, saying, "Stand up! I am just a man."

27 As he talked with him, he went in and found many who had come together,

28 and he said to them, "You know how it is unlawful for a man that is a Jew to join himself to, or come into the house of one from another nation. Yet God showed me that I should not call any man common or unclean.

29 "Therefore I came without misgivings when I was sent for. I ask therefore what reason have you sent for me."

30 Cornelius answered, "At this time four days ago I was keeping the hour of evening prayer in my house, and a man stood before me in bright apparel,

31 "and said, 'Cornelius, your prayer is heard, and your alms are known in the sight of God.

32 'Therefore send to Joppa, and call to yourself Simon, who is surnamed Peter, who is lodging in the house of Simon, a tanner who lives by the sea."

33 'Therefore, I immediately sent to you. It is good that you have come. Now therefore we are all here present in the sight of God to hear all things that have been commanded you by the Lord.'"

34 So Peter replied, "I see that it is true that God is no respecter of persons.

35 "In every nation the one who fears Him and does what is right in His sight is acceptable to Him.

36 "The word that He sent to the children of Israel, preaching good tidings of peace through Jesus Christ who is Lord of all,

37 "the message you yourselves know, which was published through-out all Judea, beginning from Galilee after the baptism that John preached

38 "concerning Jesus of Nazareth, how God anointed Him with the Holy Spirit and with power. He went about doing good and heal-ing all that were oppressed by the devil, for God was with Him.

39 "We are witnesses of all of these things that He did both in the country of the Jews, and in Jerusalem, who also killed Him, hanging Him on a tree.

40 "However, God raised Him up the third day and provided for Him to be made manifest,

41 "not to all the people, but to witnesses who were chosen before by God, even to us, who ate and drank with Him after He rose from the dead.

42 "He charged us to preach to the people and to testify that this is He who was ordained by God to be the Judge of the living and the dead.

43 "To him all the prophets bear witness that through His name every one that believes in Him will receive the remission of sins."

44 While Peter was still speaking this message, the Holy Spirit fell on all of those who heard the word.

45 So those of the circumcision who came with Peter were amazed because the gift of the Holy Spirit was poured out on the Gentiles.

46 For they heard them speak with tongues and magnify God. Then Peter said,

47 "Can any man forbid water that these should not be baptized who have received the Holy Spirit just as we did?"

48 So he commanded for them to be baptized in the name of Jesus Christ. Then they beseeched him to stay for a number of days.

The Vision of Cornelius

Acts 10:1-8: This is the historic beginning of a whole new phase of the church age as the Gentiles are offered the gospel of salvation. It begins with an angelic visitation that gives specific directions. Such clear instructions from heaven usually come because of the difficulty of the task or the importance of it. In this case, the difficulty was for the Jewish believers to understand this great purpose of God to offer His salvation to all nations. In many ways and at many times the Lord expressed His resolve to redeem all nations, but it was a stretch for any Jew to actually take the gospel to the Gentiles. It took one of such extraordinary faith like Peter to cross this barrier. This is likely why Jesus gave him the keys to the kingdom as He did in Matthew 17. Although Peter could be prone to great mistakes, he would also be willing to take great leaps of faith.

In verse 3, it says that Cornelius saw in an "open vision" the angelic messenger. There are visions that you see with "the eyes of your heart," which are more internal, and then there are those that are external and are more like watching a cinema screen, which are referred to as "open visions." This one was obviously of that nature.

Peter Goes to the Gentiles

10:9-48: To prepare Peter to go to the Gentiles with the gospel, the Lord gave him an open vision that challenges him to do something he has never done—eat food that was deemed unclean under the Law. The Lord did not tell Peter to eat what was unclean, but what He had cleansed—*it was no longer unclean.* As is often the case in prophetic revelation, the Lord was not just concerned about food here, but was using it as a metaphor. The cross has the power to cleanse and redeem anyone from any nation.

Though the main point of this is that people can be cleansed by the New Covenant, but so can food. Those who do what we are warned against in places like Colossians 2—making the eating or not eating of certain foods or other external rituals and performance a basis for our relationship to God, is a fundamental departure from the power of the cross and our New Covenant with God. Such doctrines and those who promote them are false and must be rejected.

It is noteworthy that the Lord would open such an important door for the gospel with a Roman centurion. It was a centurion about which Jesus had said that He had not seen such great a faith in all of Israel, because he believed Jesus could heal his servant just by saying a word, understanding what it meant to be under authority. The training of a soldier to understand authority is obviously a great help in understanding faith.

NOTES

THE BOOK OF
ACTS
Acts 11

The Gentiles Are Received Into the Fellowship of the Church

1   The apostles and the brethren who were in Judea heard that the Gentiles had also received the word of God.

2   So when Peter returned to Jerusalem, those who were of the circumcision challenged him, saying,

3   "You went to uncircumcised men and ate with them?"

4   So Peter explained the matter to them in order, replying,

5   "I was in the city of Joppa praying, and in a trance I saw a vision of a certain vessel descending that was like a great sheet let down from heaven by the four corners, and it came to me.

6   "When I had focused my eyes on it, I saw the four footed beasts of the earth, wild beasts, creeping things, and birds of the air.

7   "I then heard a voice saying to me, 'Arise Peter! Kill and eat.'

8   "I replied, 'No Lord. Nothing common or unclean has ever entered into my mouth.'

9   "But the voice answered the second time out of heaven, 'What God has cleansed, do not consider unclean.'

10 "This was done three times, and then it was drawn up again into heaven.

11 "Then, immediately three men were standing before the house in which we were staying, having been sent from Caesarea to me.

12 "And the Spirit told me to go with them without misgivings. These six brethren also accompanied me, and we entered into the man's house.

13 "He told us how he had seen the angel standing in his house, who said to him, 'Send to Joppa, and find Simon, whose surname is Peter,

14 "who will speak to you words by which you and your household will be saved.

15 "As I began to speak the Holy Spirit fell on them just as on us at the beginning.

16 "Then I remembered the word of the Lord, how He said, 'John indeed baptized with water, but you will be baptized with the Holy Spirit.'

17 "If then God gave to them the same gift as He did also to us when we believed on the Lord Jesus Christ, who was I to withstand God?"

18 When they heard these things, they held their peace, and glorified God, saying, "Then God has granted to the Gentiles the repentance that leads to life."

The Gentiles Stream to the Salvation of God

19 Then those who were scattered abroad because of the persecution that arose after Stephen traveled as far as Phoenicia, and Cyprus, and Antioch, speaking the word only to Jews.

20 There were some of them, men of Cyprus and Cyrene, who when they had come to Antioch, spoke to the Greeks also, preaching to them the Lord Jesus.

21 The hand of the Lord was with them, so that a great number believed and turned to the Lord.

22 When the report concerning them came to the church in Jerusalem, they sent out Barnabas to go as far as Antioch.

23 When he had come and witnessed the grace of God, he rejoiced and exhorted them all to with a single purpose of heart cleave to the Lord,

24 for he was a good man, and full of the Holy Spirit and faith. So many people were added to the Lord.

Barnabas Finds Saul and Brings Him to Antioch

25 Then Barnabas went to Tarsus to look for Saul,

26 and when he had found him, he brought him to Antioch. For a whole year they gathered together with the church there, and taught many people. The disciples were first called Christians in Antioch.

The Famine Prophesied

27 Now during these days prophets came from Jerusalem to Antioch.

28 One of them named Agabus, stood up and signified by the Spirit that there should be a great famine all over the world, which came to pass in the days of Claudius.

29 The disciples, every man according to his ability, determined to send relief to the brethren that were in Judea,

30 which they did, sending it to the elders by the hand of Barnabas and Saul.

The Gentiles Are Received Into the Fellowship of the Church

Acts 11:1-18: This chapter marks the changing of the church age from a completely Jewish movement to what would be a light of salvation of the whole world. The Lord used an angelic visitation, a trance, and the voice of the Holy Spirit to open the hearts of His people to what was clearly written in the Scriptures. This prophetic revelation did not establish the doctrine of the church on this issue but illuminated it. Even though all of the doctrines the church is built on are revealed in Scripture, sometimes it takes revelation from the Spirit to see them.

The Gentiles Stream to the Salvation of God

11:19-24: Those who first preached the gospel to the Greeks at Antioch were not apostles, but just common brethren who did this on their own. It is noteworthy that they felt free enough to do this. This reveals the remarkable liberty that the first-century church enjoyed, an obvious reason why it thrived as it did.

This also indicates again how when a significant movement of the Holy Spirit began it was the custom of the apostles and elders to send apostles, prophets, and teachers to help ground and strengthen the work.

Barnabas Finds Saul and Brings Him to Antioch

11:25-26: These two short verses describe what must have taken months for Barnabas to do, traveling all the way to Tarsus by ship, then finding Saul, and bringing him back to Antioch. It also reveals an important principle in missions—usually our own destiny is linked to someone else who we must be joined to in the mission if we are going to be promoted to our own ultimate calling.

The Famine Prophesied

11:27-30: It is noteworthy that the way the disciples responded to the prophecy when a famine was going to come upon the whole world was not to hoard, but to give—they took up an offering for the relief of the church in Judea. This remains the best way to prepare for difficulties—put our treasure in heaven where no earthly conditions can touch it.

NOTES

THE BOOK OF
ACTS
Acts 12

James Killed, Peter Arrested

1 About that time Herod the king determined to attack certain members of the church.

2 So he had James the brother of John killed with the sword.

3 When he saw that this pleased the Jews, he proceeded to seize Peter during the days of unleavened bread.

4 He had put him in prison and delivered him to four squads of soldiers to guard him and intended after the Passover to bring him before the people.

5 Peter therefore was kept in the prison, but prayer was made earnestly by the church to God for him.

6 When Herod was about to bring him forth, the same night Peter was sleeping between two soldiers, bound with two chains, and there were more guards at the door of the prison.

7 Then an angel of the Lord stood next to Peter, and a light shone into the cell, and he struck Peter on the side to wake him up, saying, "Get up quickly," and his chains fell off of his hands.

8 The angel then said to him, "Gird yourself and put on your sandals," which he did. Then the angel said to him, "Wrap your cloak about yourself, and follow me."

9 So he followed him out, but did not know that what was done by the angel was real, but thought that he was seeing a vision.

10 When they were past the first and the second guard, they came to the iron-gate that leads into the city, which opened to them

by itself. So they went out, and as they walked down a street, the angel departed from him.

11 When Peter had come to himself, he said, "Now I know that it is true that the Lord has sent his angel and delivered me from the hand of Herod and from the expectation of the Jews."

12 When he had considered the thing, he came to the house of Mary the mother of John, whose surname was Mark, where many were gathered together praying.

13 When he knocked at the door of the gate, a maid came to answer, named Rhoda.

14 When she heard Peter's voice, she did not open the gate because of her joy, but ran in, and told everyone that Peter stood outside the gate.

15 They said to her, "You are mad." But she confidently affirmed that it was true. So they said, "It is his angel."

16 Peter continued knocking, and when they had opened, they saw him and were amazed.

17 Beckoning them with his hand to be silent, he told them how the Lord had freed him from the prison, and he said, "Tell these things to James and to the brethren." So he departed.

18 Now as soon as it was day, there was no small stir among the soldiers as to what could have become of Peter.

19 When Herod asked for him to be brought, and they did not find him, he had the guards led away *to be executed.* He then went down from Judea to Caesarea and tarried there.

Herod's Death

20 Now he was very angry with the people of Tyre and Sidon, and they came with one accord to him, and having befriended Blastus, the king's chamberlain, they asked for peace, because their country was fed by the king's country.

21 So on a set day Herod arrayed himself in royal apparel and sat on the throne and made a speech to them.

22 The people shouted, "The voice of a god and not a man."

23 Immediately an angel of the Lord struck him because he did not give glory to God, and he was eaten by worms and died.

24 So the word of God grew and multiplied.

25 Barnabas and Saul returned from Jerusalem, when they had fulfilled their administration, taking with them John whose surname was Mark.

James Killed, Peter Arrested

Acts 12:1-19: The Lord allowed the Apostle James to be killed so that the church would learn to pray for their leaders. They prayed earnestly for Peter, and he was delivered. Even so, too many are still being lost for the lack of prayer on their behalf. Every Christian is a target of the enemy, but leaders are a special focus of attack, and we do need to offer special and continuous prayer for them.

It is noteworthy that when Peter came to the door of the house where the church was praying for him, they had an easier time believing that it was his angel than him. There is much evidence that the early church had considerable interchange with angels to the point where it was common. As Paul would later write, some even entertained angels without knowing it.

That they would think the angel at the door was Peter's angel rather than him is because angels that are specifically assigned to us take on our appearance. This is why many people today who have supernatural encounters with what appears to be people they recognize are really encountering their angel.

Herod's Death

12:20-25: All leaders are in jeopardy of judgment if they allow people to start worshiping them and do not give glory to God.

NOTES

THE BOOK OF
ACTS
Acts 13

First Missionary Journey

1   Now there were prophets and teachers at the church in Antioch,
    Barnabas, and Simeon who was called Niger, and Lucius of Cyrene,
    and Manaen the foster-brother of Herod the tetrarch, and Saul.

2   As they ministered to the Lord and fasted, the Holy Spirit said,
    "Separate Barnabas and Saul for the work to which I have called
    them."

3   Then, when they had fasted and prayed and laid their hands on
    them, they sent them away.

4   So, they being sent forth by the Holy Spirit went down to Seleucia
    and from there they sailed to Cyprus.

5   When they were at Salamis, they proclaimed the word of God in the
    synagogues of the Jews, and they had John Mark as their attendant.

Witness to the Proconsul

6   When they had gone through the whole island as far as Paphos,
    they found a certain sorcerer, a false prophet, who was a Jew
    named Bar-Jesus.

7   He was with the proconsul, Sergius Paulus, a man of understand-
    ing who called Barnabas and Saul to come to him and sought to
    hear the word of God.

8   Elymas the sorcerer (for this is his name by interpretation) opposed
    them, seeking to turn the proconsul away from the faith.

9   So Saul, who is also called Paul, being filled with the Holy Spirit,
    fastened his eyes on him

10 and said, "O you who are full of all deceit and evil, you son of the devil, you enemy of all righteousness, will you not cease to pervert the straight ways of the Lord?

11 "Now the hand of the Lord is upon you, and you will be blind and not see the sun for a season." Immediately a mist and a darkness fell upon him, and he went off to seek someone to lead him by the hand.

12 When the proconsul saw what was done he believed, being astonished at the teaching of the Lord.

Witness to the Jews

13 Then Paul and his company set sail from Paphos, and came to Perga in Pamphylia, and John departed from them and returned to Jerusalem.

14 So they, passing through from Perga, came to Antioch of Pisidia, and they went into the synagogue on the Sabbath day and sat down.

15 After the reading of the Law and the Prophets the rulers of the synagogue sent to them, saying, "Brethren, if you have a word of exhortation for the people, speak."

16 Paul stood up, and beckoning with his hand said, "Men of Israel, and you that fear God, listen:

17 "The God of Israel chose our fathers, and exalted the people when they sojourned in the land of Egypt, and with a mighty arm He led them out of it.

18 "For about the time of forty years He bore them in the wilderness like a nursing-father.

19 "When He had destroyed seven nations in the land of Canaan, He gave them their land for an inheritance. This all took about four hundred and fifty years.

20 "And after these things He gave them judges until Samuel the prophet.

21 "After this they asked for a king. So God gave them Saul the son of Kish, a man from the tribe of Benjamin, for forty years.

22 "When He had removed him, He raised up David to be their king; to whom also He bore witness and said, '**I have found David the son of Jesse, a man after My heart, who will do all of My will**' **(I Samuel 13:14).**

23 "From this man's seed God has, just as He promised, brought to Israel a Savior, Jesus,

24 "after John had first preached the baptism of repentance to all the people of Israel before His coming.

25 "After John had fulfilled his course, he said, 'Who do you suppose that I am? I am not Him, but there comes One after me the shoes of whose feet I am not worthy to untie.'

26 "Brethren, children of Abraham, and those among you that fear God, it is to us that the word of this salvation is sent to.

27 "For those who dwell in Jerusalem, and their rulers, because they did not recognize Him, nor understand the voices of the prophets which are read every Sabbath, fulfilled them by condemning Him.

28 "Though they found no cause worthy to put Him to death, yet they demanded of Pilate that He should be slain.

29 "When they had fulfilled all things that were written of Him, they took Him down from the tree, and laid Him in a tomb.

30 "But God raised Him from the dead,

31 "and He was seen for many days by those who came up with Him from Galilee to Jerusalem, who are now His witnesses to the people.

32 "We bring you these good tidings of the promise made to the fathers,

33 "that God has fulfilled these to His children when He raised up Jesus, just as also it is written in the second psalm, **'You are My Son, this day have I begotten You' (Psalm 2:7).**

34 "Concerning the fact that He raised Him up from the dead, to never again return to corruption, He has spoken on this also, saying, **'I will give You the holy and sure blessings of David' (Isaiah 55:3).**

35 "As is also written in another psalm, **'You will not give Your Holy One to see corruption' (Psalm 16:10).**

36 "After David had served the counsel of God in his own generation, he fell asleep, and was laid to rest with his fathers, and saw corruption,

37 "but He whom God raised up saw no corruption.

38 "Be it known to you therefore, brethren, that through this man is proclaimed to you the remission of sins,

39 "and by Him every one who believes is justified from all transgressions, from which you could not be justified by the Law of Moses.

40 "Beware therefore, lest that come upon you which is spoken in the Prophets:

41 **'Behold, you scoffers, wonder, and perish; because I will do a work in your days, a work which you will in no way believe, even if one declares it to you'" (Habakkuk 1:5).**

42 As they left they asked that these words might be spoken to them again the next Sabbath.

43 Now when the synagogue broke up, many of the Jews and the devout proselytes followed Paul and Barnabas, who, speaking to them, urged them to continue in the grace of God.

44 The next Sabbath almost the whole city was gathered together to hear the word of God.

45 When the Jews saw the multitudes, they were filled with jealousy, and contradicted the things that were spoken by Paul, and even blasphemed.

Turning to the Gentiles

46 So Paul and Barnabas spoke out boldly, and said, "It was necessary that the word of God should first be spoken to you. Seeing that you reject it, and judge yourselves unworthy of eternal life, we will turn to the Gentiles.

47 "For this is what the Lord commanded us, saying, **'I have sent you to be a light for the Gentiles, that you should declare salvation to the uttermost part of the earth'" (Isaiah 49:6).**

48 As the Gentiles heard this, they were rejoicing, and glorified the word of God, and as many as were ordained to eternal life believed.

49 So the word of the Lord was spreading abroad throughout the whole region.

50 However, the Jews persuaded the devout women of the nobility and the chief men of the city, and stirred up a persecution against Paul and Barnabas, and drove them from their borders.

51 So they shook off the dust of their feet against them, and came to Iconium,

52 but the disciples were filled with joy, and with the Holy Spirit.

First Missionary Journey

Acts 13:1-5: There were five in Antioch who were prophets, teachers, or both, and were ministering to the Lord together when the new apostles were commissioned. Prophets and teachers must learn to serve the Lord together before there can be a birth of true apostolic ministry.

Since the founding of the church, apostles have been sent to follow up a work begun by others, but this is the first recorded missionary journey of this nature that apostles had been sent on. The rest of the Book of Acts is mostly about how this type of mission was carried out by Paul and his coworkers.

Witness to the Proconsul

13:6-12: The apostles did not just demonstrate power to be a witness of the gospel, but also to silence the enemy. It is noteworthy that this is the way their first missionary journey began.

Witness to the Jews

13:13-45: Paul and Barnabas obeyed by taking the gospel to the Jews first. They were to receive it first as the ones who had the first covenant with God that was being replaced by a new one, and as the ones who had been the custodians of the Word of God, and the spiritual seed that would bring forth Christ. As we see here and was often the case, the rejection of the gospel of the New Covenant by the Jews was for the same reason that Jesus had been crucified—the jealousy of the leaders.

Turning to the Gentiles

13:46-52: From this time on, the gospel was primarily bearing fruit among the Gentiles. The gospel was almost

always persecuted, but it seemed to spread even more under persecution than when they enjoyed peace.

NOTES

THE BOOK OF
ACTS
Acts 14

Multitudes Believe

1   At Iconium they entered together into the synagogue of the Jews to speak, and a great multitude of both Jews and Greeks believed.

2   However, the Jews that were disobedient stirred up the souls of the Gentiles and turned them against the brethren.

3   Even so, they tarried there for a long time speaking boldly of the Lord, who bore witness to the word of His grace by granting signs and wonders to be done by their hands.

4   However, the people of the city were divided, part siding with the Jews and part with the apostles.

5   Then there was a plot made by the Gentiles and their rulers, along with the Jews, to treat them shamefully and to stone them.

6   When they became aware of it, they fled to the cities of Lycaonia, Lystra and Derbe, and the region around them,

7   and there they preached the gospel.

8   In Lystra there sat a certain man who was crippled in his feet from his mother's womb and had never walked.

9   When he heard Paul speak, Paul fastened his eyes upon him, seeing that he had faith to be healed,

10 said with a loud voice, "Stand upright on your feet." He immediately leaped up and walked.

The Apostles Called Gods

11 When the multitude saw what Paul had done, they raised their voices, saying in the speech of Lycaonia, "The gods have come down to us in the likeness of men."

12 So they called Barnabas, Jupiter, and Paul, Mercury, because he was the main speaker.

13 The priest of Jupiter, whose temple was outside of the city, brought oxen and garlands to the gates to sacrifice them with the multitudes.

14 When Barnabas and Paul heard of it, they tore their garments and ran into the multitude, crying out saying,

15 "Sirs, why do you do these things? We also are men with like passions as you and bring you good news, that you should turn from these vain things to the living God, who made the heaven and the earth and the sea, and all that is in them,

16 "who in the generations gone by allowed all the nations to walk in their own ways,

17 "and yet He did not leave Himself without witness, in that He did good and gave you rains from heaven and fruitful seasons, filling your hearts with food and gladness."

18 With these declarations they still barely restrained the multitudes from sacrificing to them.

Paul Stoned

19 Then the Jews from Antioch and Iconium came down, and they persuaded the multitudes. Then they stoned Paul, and dragged him out of the city believing that he was dead.

20 As the disciples stood around him, he rose up, and entered into the city, and on the next day he went with Barnabas to Derbe.

21 When they had preached the gospel to that city, and had made many disciples, they returned to Lystra, and to Iconium, and to Antioch,

22 strengthening the souls of the disciples, exhorting them to continue in the faith, and declaring to them that it is through many tribulations that we must enter into the kingdom of God.

23 When they had appointed elders in every church, and had prayed with fasting, they commended them to the Lord on whom they had believed.

24 Then they passed through Pisidia and came to Pamphylia.

25 When they had spoken the word in Perga, they went down to Attalia,

26 and then they sailed to Antioch, from where they had been committed to the grace of God for the work which they had fulfilled.

27 When they arrived and had gathered the church together, they rehearsed all of the things that God had done through them, how He had opened a door of faith to the Gentiles.

28 So they stayed there for a short time with the disciples.

Multitudes Believe

Acts 14:1-10: As the Lord Jesus had prophesied, His gospel would bring a sword of division in many places, and as we see here, the greater the success we have leading people to the Lord, the more persecution we can expect.

The Apostles Called Gods

14:11-18: Great miracles can cause many to believe, but if sound teaching is not quickly added to the belief of those who come to the Lord because of miracles, they can be led astray again very fast. A multitude can become a mob quickly, just as the same ones who welcomed Jesus to Jerusalem crying "Hosanna," would five days later be calling for Him to be crucified. For this same reason, political polls can make big swings up and down. We should never be too excited when the multitudes are favorable or discouraged when they are not, but rather get our encouragement from the Lord and resolve that regardless of what the people think, we will remain faithful to the truth.

Paul Stoned

14:19-28: Miracles demand a response if those who witness

them do not turn to the Lord, or they will turn against Him. This was true even with Jesus. The more powerful His miracles were, the greater the jealousy and the greater the persecution. So it was with the apostles and is with His messengers to this day. However, the miracles did help to establish the faith of the new believers on the power of God, and not just the wisdom of men.

In verse 22, Paul exhorts the believers that it is through many tribulations that they must enter the kingdom. This is a basic principle—our trials are a doorway to the kingdom and for us to get closer to the King. It will also be through "the great tribulation" at the end of the age that the whole world enters into the kingdom. In every trial, look for the door to the kingdom.

In verse 23, we see that even though no believer had known the Lord for more than a few months, the apostles appointed elders in every church. Even immature leadership is better than no leadership.

NOTES

THE BOOK OF
ACTS
Acts 15

The First Heresy

1   Then certain men came down from Judea to teach the brethren, saying, "Unless you are circumcised after the custom of Moses you cannot be saved."

2   When Paul and Barnabas had no small dissension with them, challenging their teaching, the brethren appointed Paul and Barnabas, and certain others to go up to Jerusalem to ask the apostles and elders about this matter.

3   Being sent on their way by the church, they passed through both Phoenicia and Samaria, declaring the news of the conversion of the Gentiles, causing great joy to all the brethren.

4   When they arrived at Jerusalem, they were received by the church and the apostles and elders, and they rehearsed all of the things that God had done through them.

5   Then some of the sect of the Pharisees who believed rose up saying, "It is necessary to circumcise them and to charge them to keep the Law of Moses."

The Jerusalem Council

6   So the apostles and the elders gathered together to consider this matter.

7   When there had been much debate and questioning, Peter rose up and said to them, "Brethren, you know that a long time ago God

made a choice among you, that by my mouth the Gentiles should hear the word of the gospel and believe.

8 "God, who knows the heart, bore them witness, giving them the Holy Spirit, even as He did to us,

9 "and He made no distinction between us and them, cleansing their hearts by faith.

10 "Now therefore why put God to the test, to put a yoke upon the neck of the disciples which neither our fathers nor we were able to bear?

11 "We believe that we are saved through the grace of the Lord Jesus, just as they are."

12 So the whole multitude kept silent as they listened to Barnabas and Paul rehearsing the signs and wonders God had wrought among the Gentiles through them.

13 After they had finished, James answered, saying, "Brethren, listen to me.

14 "Simon has rehearsed how God first visited the Gentiles, to take from among them a people for His name.

15 "To this the words of the prophets agree, as it is written,

16 **'After these things I will return, and I will rebuild the tabernacle of David which is fallen, and I will again build upon the ruins of it, and I will establish it,**

17 **'so that the rest of mankind may seek the Lord, and all of the Gentiles, upon whom My name is called,**

18 **'says the Lord, who makes these things known from ancient times' (Amos 9:11-12).**

19 "Therefore, it is my judgment that we do not trouble those from among the Gentiles who turn to God,

20 "but that we write to them that they abstain from that which is sacrificed to idols and from fornication and from what is strangled and from blood.

21 "For Moses has had some in every city who preach him, being read in the synagogues every Sabbath, even from ancient times."

The First Decree

22 Then it seemed good to the apostles and the elders, along with the whole church, to choose men of their company, and send them to Antioch with Paul and Barnabas, namely, Judas called Barsabbas, and Silas, chief men among the brethren,

23 and they sent with them a letter stating,

> **"The apostles, elders, and brethren, to the brethren who are of the Gentiles in Antioch and Syria and Cilicia, greetings.**
>
> 24 **"Because we have heard that certain ones who went out from us have troubled you with their teachings, subverting your souls, these to whom we gave no such instructions,**
>
> 25 **"it seemed good to us, having become of one accord, to choose men and send them to you with our beloved Barnabas and Paul,**
>
> 26 **"men that have risked their lives for the name of our Lord Jesus Christ.**
>
> 27 **"We have sent therefore Judas and Silas, who themselves also shall tell you the same things by word of mouth.**
>
> 28 **"For it seemed good to the Holy Spirit and to us to lay upon you no greater burden than these necessary things:**
>
> 29 **"that you abstain from things sacrificed to idols and from blood and from things strangled and from fornication, from which if you keep yourselves, it shall be well with you. Farewell."**

30 So when they were dismissed, they came down to Antioch; and having gathered the multitude together, they delivered the letter.

31 When they had read it, they rejoiced at its consolation.

32 So Judas and Silas, being themselves also prophets, exhorted the brethren with many words and confirmed them.

33 After they had spent some time there, they were dismissed in peace from the brethren to return to those that had sent them forth.

34 But it seemed good to Silas to remain there.

35 So Paul and Barnabas tarried in Antioch, teaching and preaching the word of the Lord, with many others also.

Paul and Barnabas Separate

36 After some days Paul said to Barnabas, "Let us return now and visit the brethren in every city where we proclaimed the word of the Lord and see how they are doing."

37 So Barnabas wanted to take with them John, who was called Mark.

38 But Paul did not want to take him with them because he had deserted them in Pamphylia and did not go with them to the work.

39 Then there arose a sharp contention, so that they parted from one another, and Barnabas took Mark with him and sailed away to Cyprus.

40 But Paul chose Silas and went forth, being commended by the brethren to the grace of the Lord.

41 So he went through Syria and Cilicia, confirming the churches.

The First Heresy

Acts 15:1-5: This is one of the most important chapters in the New Testament. The first heresy to arise in church history was from the religious sect that sought to turn the young church back to keeping the Law of Moses for righteousness. This would have cut the church off from the power of the cross of Jesus that is alone the basis of our righteousness. We will never be acceptable to the Father because of how good we've been, but we are all acceptable because of the sacrifice Jesus made for our redemption. This does not mean that we can continue in sin, because the redeemed have been bought with a price so that they should no longer abide in sin, but rather abide in the One in whom there is no sin. Only by abiding in Him do we have the power to overcome sin, but only by the cross of Jesus do we have forgiveness of sin.

The Jerusalem Council

15:6-21: This council of the apostles and elders in Jerusalem is the only one in church history that represented the entire leadership of the church. Peter was given the keys to the kingdom, and he used them to open the door of faith to both the Jews and the Gentiles. Here he relates that he had been the one to open the door of faith to the Gentiles, and he resolutely and successfully challenged the teaching of the need for the Gentiles to come under the yoke of the Law, saving the church from this devastating heresy.

The First Decree

15:22-35: This is the only apostolic decree in the Scriptures. All others in church history that presume such authority have challenges that negate them. Should we not therefore consider this one, which beckons the church to abide in the simplicity of devotion to Christ for its righteousness, the most important decree in history and possibly the only valid one ever given to the church? Its intent is to set the Gentile believers free from the yoke of the Law, yet nearly 2,000 years afterwards this is still one of the primary conflicts afflicting the church. When we see this legalism creeping in, this is the chapter we can refer to as a basis for our freedom. After this, the entire Book of Galatians is basically about this issue.

Paul and Barnabas Separate

15:36-41: Even mature apostles can have conflict and separate from one another. However, this is the last time we hear of the work of Barnabas in Scripture, and the work of Paul becomes the focus of the rest of the Book of Acts. Some have asserted that as we see in verse 40, Paul and Silas were commended by the brethren to the work, which implies that Barnabas and Mark were not. The Lord has delegated authority to His church, which must be respected if we expect the full blessing of the Lord.

NOTES

THE BOOK OF
ACTS
Acts 16

Timothy Joins Paul

1 Paul then came to Derbe and to Lystra, and a certain disciple was there named Timothy. He was the son of a Jewess that believed, but his father was a Greek.

2 He had a good reputation with all of the brethren that were at Lystra and Iconium.

3 Paul wanted him to travel with him, so he took and had him circumcised because of the Jews that were in those parts, for they all knew that his father was a Greek.

4 As they went on their way through the cities, they delivered to the believers the decrees to keep which had been ordained by the apostles and elders in Jerusalem.

5 So the churches were strengthened in the faith and increased in number daily.

6 From there they went through the region of Phrygia and Galatia, having been forbidden by the Holy Spirit to speak the word in Asia.

7 When they had come over close to Mysia, they wanted to go into Bithynia, but the Spirit of Jesus would not allow them to.

8 So they passed by Mysia and came down to Troas.

9 Then a vision appeared to Paul in the night of a man of Macedonia standing and beseeching him, saying, "Come over into Macedonia and help us."

10 When he had seen the vision, immediately we sought to go forth into Macedonia, concluding that God had called us to preach the gospel to them.

11 So, setting sail from Troas, we made a straight course to Samothrace, and the day following to Neapolis;

12 and from there to Philippi, which is a city of Macedonia, the first of the district, a Roman colony, and we remained in this city waiting for a number of days.

Birth of the Church at Philippi

13 On the Sabbath day we went out of the gate to the riverside where we expected to find a place to pray. When we sat down we began to speak to the women that were gathered together.

14 A certain woman named Lydia, a seller of purple in the city of Thyatira, one who worshiped God, heard us, and her heart had been opened by the Lord to give heed to the things that were spoken by Paul.

15 When she and her household had been baptized, she entreated us, saying, "If you have judged me to be faithful to the Lord, come into my house and stay." So she prevailed upon us.

The Spirit of Divination

16 It came about as we were going to the place of prayer, that a certain maid having a spirit of divination met us who was bringing her masters much income by her soothsaying.

17 She started following after Paul and us, crying out and saying, "These men are servants of the Most High God, who proclaim to you the way of salvation."

18 She did this for many days, but Paul, being troubled by this, turned and said to the spirit, "I charge you in the name of Jesus Christ to come out of her," and it came out immediately.

Paul and Silas Imprisoned

19 When her masters saw that the source of their income was gone, they laid hold of Paul and Silas, and dragged them into the marketplace before the rulers.

20 When they had brought them to the magistrates, they said, "These men, being Jews, do exceedingly trouble our city,

21 "and teach customs that it is not lawful for us to receive or to observe, as we are Romans."

22 So the multitude rose up together against them, and the magistrates tore their garments off them and commanded them to be beaten with rods.

23 When they had laid many stripes upon them, they cast them into prison, charging the jailor to keep them securely,

24 who, having received such a charge, cast them into the inner prison, and made their feet fast in the stocks.

25 At about midnight Paul and Silas were praying and singing hymns to God, and the prisoners were listening to them.

26 Then suddenly there was a great earthquake, so that the foundation of the prison was shaken, and immediately all the doors were opened, and every one's shackles were loosed.

27 The jailor, being awakened, and seeing the prison doors open, drew his sword and was about to kill himself, supposing that the prisoners had escaped,

28 but Paul cried with a loud voice, saying, "Do yourself no harm! We are all here."

Philippian Jailer Saved

29 Then he called for lights and ran into the prison trembling in fear and fell down before Paul and Silas,

30 and brought them out and said, "Sirs, what must I do to be saved?"

31 They said, "Believe on the Lord Jesus, and you shall be saved, you and your household."

32 So they spoke the word of the Lord to him, along with all that were in his house.

33 He took them the same hour of the night and washed their wounds, and then he was immediately baptized with his whole house.

34 Then he brought them up into his home, and set food before them, and rejoiced greatly, with his house, having believed in God.

35 When it was day the magistrates sent the sergeants, saying, "Let those men go."

36 The jailor reported the words to Paul, saying, "The magistrates have sent to let you go. Now therefore, come out, and go in peace."

37 Paul said to them, "They have beaten us publicly, uncondemned men who are Romans, and have cast us into prison, and do they now let us go in secret? No, but let them come themselves and bring us out."

38 When the sergeants reported these words to the magistrates, they became afraid when they heard that they were Romans,

39 and they came personally and entreated them. When they had brought them out, they asked them to leave the city.

40 So they left the prison and entered into the house of Lydia, and when they had seen the brethren, they comforted them and departed.

Timothy Joins Paul

Acts 16:1-12: Timothy seems to have taken the place of Mark who Paul and Barnabas had taken with them on their first missionary journey. Because making disciples was fundamental to the Great Commission, the apostles and the leaders of the early church were constantly seeking those who they could impart their wisdom and experience to who would continue the work after them. Timothy became that primary disciple for Paul.

Birth of the Church at Philippi

16:13-15: The church at Philippi was born because a woman merchant believed along with her household. Women in business are prominent in the New Testament, not only supporting the ministry of Jesus, but also in the promulgation of the gospel. They still are the primary drive behind missions, the preaching of the gospel, and the ministry of the body of Christ.

The Spirit of Divination

16:16-18: It is assumed by many that the spirit in this girl was promoting the message of the apostles in a mocking way, but this is not necessarily the case. It is common for those with a wrong spirit to try to actually promote the work of God, not to help it, but rather to have an association with it in order to gain access to the inner circle and begin to control it. This is so they can bring confusion or disruption later, even though they themselves may think they are an important aid to the work. Paul discerned the source of this girl's promotion of the gospel, would not tolerate it, and neither should any who are in authority in the church.

Paul and Silas Imprisoned

16:19-28: It was because the owners of the slave girl, who had the spirit of divination, saw that their chance for profit was lost that they began the persecution of Paul and Silas. This is common throughout the New Testament and church history. When persecution begins, it is seldom about the doctrine as much as the teaching is seen as having a negative impact on someone's profit.

Philippian Jailer Saved

16:29-40: This dramatic and dangerous beginning to the work in Asia was likely the reason why the Holy Spirit had prevented the apostles from preaching the gospel there until the right time. However, by having the vision from God so that they knew they were in the will of God, it enabled the apostles to rejoice in their afflictions. These would be just the beginning of the difficulties they would have in Asia, and they needed to know for sure they were in the right place. Even with this great conflict, some of the remarkable churches of the first century would be raised up in this region. This is often the case—where there is the biggest battle it is usually because of its strategic importance.

NOTES

THE BOOK OF
ACTS
Acts 17

Turning the World Upside Down

1   When they had passed through Amphipolis and Apollonia, they came to Thessalonica, where there was a synagogue of the Jews.

2   As was the custom of Paul, he went to them, and for three Sabbath days reasoned with them from the Scriptures,

3   opening them and reasoning that it was the purpose of the Christ to suffer and to rise again from the dead, and about whom Jesus he said, "I proclaim to you is the Christ."

4   Some of them were persuaded and consorted with Paul and Silas, and of the devout Greeks there was a great multitude, and of the chief women there were also many.

5   The Jews, becoming jealous, took certain vile fellows from the rabble, gathered a crowd and set the city in an uproar; and assaulting the house of Jason, they sought to bring them before the people.

6   When they did not find *the apostles*, they dragged Jason and some of the brethren before the rulers of the city, crying, "Those who have turned the world upside down have come here also, whom Jason has received.

7   "These all act contrary to the decrees of Caesar, saying that there is another King, Jesus."

8   So they stirred up the multitude and the rulers of the city when they said these things.

9   After they had taken security from Jason and the rest, they let them go.

The Noble Spirit of the Bereans

10 So the brethren immediately sent Paul and Silas away by night to Berea, and when they had come, there they went into the synagogue of the Jews.

11 Now these were more noble than those in Thessalonica. They received the word with open minds, and then examined the Scriptures daily to see whether these things were so.

12 Many of them therefore believed, along with some of the Greek women of the nobility and quite a few men.

13 When the Jews of Thessalonica heard that the word of God had been proclaimed of Paul at Berea also, they came there likewise, stirring up and troubling the multitudes.

14 So immediately the brethren sent Paul away to go as far as the sea, but Silas and Timothy remained there.

Paul at Athens

15 Those who conducted Paul brought him as far as Athens, and after receiving instructions for Silas and Timothy to join him as fast as they could, they departed.

16 Now while Paul waited for them at Athens, his spirit was provoked as he beheld the city full of idols.

17 So he reasoned in the synagogue with Jews and the devout, and in the marketplace every day with those whom he met.

18 When some of the Epicurean and Stoic philosophers encountered him, they said, "What would this babbler say?" Others said, "He seems to be a promoter of strange gods," because he preached Jesus and the resurrection.

19 So they took hold of him, and brought him to the Areopagus, saying, "Explain to us what this new teaching is that you are proclaiming.

20 "For you are bringing strange things to our ears, and we would like to know what these things mean."

21 Now all the Athenians and the strangers sojourning there, spent their time in nothing but discussing what was new.

22 So Paul stood in the midst of the Areopagus and said, "You men of Athens, in all things I perceive that you are very religious.

23 "For as I passed along and observed the objects of your worship, I found also an altar with this inscription, 'TO AN UNKNOWN GOD.' What therefore you worship in ignorance this I proclaim to you.

24 "The God who made the world and all things in it, being the Lord of heaven and earth, does not dwell in temples made with hands.

25 "Neither is He served by human hands as though He needed anything, seeing that He Himself gives to all their life, and breath, and all things.

26 "He made from one, every nation of men to dwell on all the face of the earth, having determined their appointed seasons, and the bounds of their habitation,

27 "so that they might seek God, if perhaps they might grope after Him and find Him, though He is not far from each one of us.

28 "For in Him we live and move and have our being, as even some of your own poets have said, 'For we are also His offspring.'

29 "Being then the offspring of God, we should not think that God can be compared to gold, silver, and stone, or fashioned by the art and device of man.

30 "The times of ignorance God has overlooked, but now He is commanding all men everywhere to repent,

31 "and He has appointed a day in which He will judge the world in righteousness by the man whom He has ordained, through whom He has given assurance to all men, as He has raised Him from the dead."

32 Now when they heard of the resurrection of the dead, some mocked, but others said, "We will hear from you again concerning this."

33 After this Paul went out from among them.

34 Some of the men followed him and believed. Among these there were Dionysius the Areopagite, and a woman named Damaris, and others with them.

Turning the World Upside Down

Acts 17:1-9: The birth of the church at Thessalonica was with great conflict and controversy just as was the case with most of the churches in the first century. The success of the gospel and those who preached it almost always stirred up jealousy in others from the religious community. These inevitably rose up to persecute and seek to destroy the new work. This is still the general pattern that can be expected in church planting if we are doing a true and significant work.

The officials of this great city remarked that "those who have turned the world upside down have now come here to us." This is indicative of the impact that the gospel was having throughout the world. This was done without arms or huge advertising campaigns but simply by the power of the truth.

The Noble Spirit of the Bereans

17:10-14: In contrast to those of Thessalonica, the religious community in Berea received the word with openness and then searched the Scriptures to verify what they were being taught. This is a great example of how we should approach all teaching, first being open, not fearful, but then searching the Scriptures to verify what we have heard. Here this resulted in the belief of many, and their faith would begin on a strong foundation. The noble-mindedness of the Bereans is still lauded to this day but unfortunately seems to be just as rare now as it was then.

Paul at Athens

17:15-34: Paul's discourse at Athens remains one of his most famous and most quoted, as he brilliantly used the basis of their philosophy to share with them the gospel of Jesus. However, as far as fruit for the gospel, there was very little as Athens is one of the few places Paul preached that a church was not born. The next city Paul went to was Corinth, and there he had a very different strategy, determining to preach nothing but the cross and Jesus crucified. Obviously, Paul was one of the most brilliant and learned men of his time, and some say of all-time, but he was wise enough not to care much for impressing people, but for saving them. Therefore, it seems that he abandoned the strategy of trying to use reasoning and relied on the Spirit and the power of God from that time on to promote the gospel.

NOTES

THE BOOK OF
ACTS
Acts 18

Priscilla and Aquila

1   After these things Paul departed from Athens and came to Corinth.

2   There he found a certain Jew named Aquila, a native of Pontus, who had lately come from Italy with his wife Priscilla, because Claudius had commanded all the Jews to depart from Rome. So Paul went to them,

3   and because he was of the same trade, he lodged with them, and they worked together because by trade they were tent makers.

4   So he reasoned in the synagogue every Sabbath, persuading both Jews and Greeks.

5   When Silas and Timothy came down from Macedonia, Paul devoted himself to preaching the word, testifying to the Jews that Jesus was the Christ.

6   When some began to oppose and blasphemed, he shook out his raiment and said to them, "Your blood be upon your own heads, from which I am no longer responsible. From this time on I will go to the Gentiles."

The Church at Corinth Born

7   So Paul departed from them and went into the house of a certain man named Titus Justus, who worshiped God, and whose house was joined to the synagogue.

8   Crispus, the ruler of the synagogue, also believed in the Lord with his house. So many of the Corinthians who heard believed and were baptized.

9 Then the Lord said to Paul in a night vision, "Do not be afraid, but speak, and do not hold back,

10 "for I am with you, and no man will harm you, because I have many people in this city."

11 So he dwelt there for eighteen months, teaching the word of God among them.

12 When Gallio was proconsul of Achaia, the Jews with one accord rose up against Paul and brought him before the judgment seat,

13 saying, "This man persuades men to worship God contrary to the law."

14 When Paul was about to open his mouth, Gallio said to the Jews, "If indeed it were a matter of a crime or of wickedness, O Jews, reason would dictate that I should bear with you!

15 "But if there are questions about words and names and your own law, look to it yourselves. I am not willing to be a judge of these matters."

16 So he drove them from the judgment seat.

17 Then they all laid hold of Sosthenes, the ruler of the synagogue, and beat him before the judgment seat. But Gallio did not pay attention to any of these things.

18 So Paul, having tarried after this for many days, took his leave of the brethren and sailed from there to Syria, and Priscilla and Aquila went with him. Paul had shorn his head in Cenchrea, because he had made a vow.

Paul's First Visit to Ephesus

19 So they came to Ephesus, and he left them there, but he himself entered into the synagogue and reasoned with the Jews.

20 When they asked him to abide longer, he did not consent,

21 but taking his leave of them, he said, "I will return again to you if God wills," and he set sail from Ephesus.

22 When he had landed at Caesarea he went up and saluted the church, and went down to Antioch.

23 Having spent some time there, he departed and went through the region of Galatia and Phrygia, strengthening and establishing all the disciples.

Apollos

24 Now a certain Jew named Apollos, an Alexandrian, an eloquent man, came to Ephesus, and he was mighty in the Scriptures.

25 This man had been instructed in the way of the Lord, and being fervent in spirit, he preached and taught accurately the things concerning Jesus, but he only knew about the baptism of John.

26 When he began to speak boldly in the synagogue, Priscilla and Aquila heard him, and so they took him aside and expounded to him the way of God more accurately.

27 When he was intending to pass over into Achaia, the brethren encouraged him and wrote to the disciples to receive him. When he had come, he greatly helped those who had believed through grace.

28 For he powerfully refuted the Jews, doing this publicly, showing by the Scriptures that Jesus was the Christ.

Priscilla and Aquila

Acts 18:1-6: Pricilla and Aquila would become instrumental in making further developments in the apostolic mission. They might never have met Paul if it had not been for the Roman persecution of the Jews and their removal from Rome. God causes all things to work for good. Throughout church history, persecutions are often the beginning of breakthroughs for the gospel, as we also see in this account of how persecution kept the apostles moving, spreading the word. What the devil means for evil always turns out for good if we do not stop.

The Church at Corinth Born

18:7-18: For Paul to spend eighteen months in one place was extraordinary, but it was for the purpose of raising up one of the great churches in the first century. Right after some of his greatest setbacks, beginning in Athens, Paul begins a series of great victories in his mission. Such is often the pattern in missions. In the Lord, there are no real setbacks, just learning opportunities.

Paul's First Visit to Ephesus

18:19-23: Right after Corinth, Paul briefly stops at Ephesus and begins the work there, which would also become one of the great churches of the first century. Now Paul is on a major winning streak, but Paul did not seem to recognize how important these were. This is also the typical pattern for missions—some of the greatest accomplishments may not be recognizable for many years and may not be seen by the missionary at all. Missionaries must therefore simply be obedient and trust the Lord for the fruit.

Apollos

18:24-28: Apollos emerged as one of the great teachers of the first century. Pricilla and Aquila saw the gift in Apollos and helped him become even more effective in strengthening the disciples. One of the great needs is for such teachers to follow apostolic missions to help the disciples sink their roots deep into sound doctrine. The failure to use this strategy has resulted in making many converts, but not many disciples who go on to become Christ-like and live with a biblical worldview.

NOTES

THE BOOK OF
ACTS
Acts 19

The Holy Spirit at Ephesus

1 While Apollos was at Corinth, Paul having passed through the upper country, came to Ephesus, and he found some disciples there.

2 So he said to them, "Did you receive the Holy Spirit when you believed?" They replied, "No. We did not even hear that there was a Holy Spirit."

3 He then asked, "Into what then were you baptized?" They said, "Into John's baptism."

4 Paul then said, "John baptized with the baptism of repentance, saying to the people that they should believe in Him that would come after him, that is, in Jesus."

5 So when they heard this, they were baptized into the name of the Lord Jesus.

6 Then Paul laid his hands upon them and the Holy Spirit came on them, and they spoke with tongues and prophesied.

7 There were in all about twelve men.

8 Then he entered into the synagogue, and spoke boldly for three months, reasoning and persuading about the things concerning the kingdom of God.

The School of Tyrannus

9 When some became hardened and disobedient, speaking evil of the Way before the multitude, Paul departed from them and

separated the disciples. Then he began teaching daily in the school of Tyrannus.

10 This continued for two years, so that all who dwelt in Asia heard the word of the Lord, both Jews and Greeks.

11 God also wrought special miracles by the hands of Paul,

12 so that handkerchiefs or aprons were carried away from him, and when they touched the sick they were healed, and the evil spirits departed from them.

The Jewish Exorcists

13 Then certain Jewish exorcists took it upon themselves to use the name of Jesus with those who had the evil spirits, saying, "I adjure you by Jesus whom Paul preaches."

14 There were seven sons of one Sceva, a Jewish chief priest, who did this.

15 But the evil spirit answered and said to them, "Jesus I know, and Paul I know, but who are you?"

16 Then the man who had the evil spirit leaped on them and overpowered them, so that they fled out of that house naked and wounded.

17 This became known to all who dwelt in Ephesus, both Jews and Greeks, and a great fear fell upon them all so that the name of the Lord Jesus was magnified.

18 Many of those who had believed came, confessing, and declaring their evil deeds.

19 So a great number who had practiced magical arts brought their books together and burned them in the sight of all, and they counted the price of them and found it to be fifty thousand pieces of silver.

20 So the word of the Lord grew mightily and prevailed.

21 Now after these things, Paul passed through Macedonia and Achaia and purposed in his spirit to go to Jerusalem, saying, "After I have been there, I must also see Rome."

22 So he sent two of those who ministered with him into Macedonia, Timothy and Erastus, but he himself stayed in Asia for a while.

Riots for Diana

23 At about that time there arose a great controversy concerning the Way.

24 *This began with* a certain man named Demetrius, a silversmith, who made silver shrines for Diana, and brought a lot of business to the craftsmen.

25 These he gathered together with the workmen of like occupation, and said, "Sirs, you know that by this business we have our source of wealth.

26 "You see and hear, that not only at Ephesus, but almost throughout all Asia, this Paul has persuaded and turned away many people, saying that they are not gods that are made with hands.

27 "Not only is there danger that this trade of ours come into disrepute, but also that the temple of the great goddess Diana will be made of no account, and that she should even be deposed from her magnificence whom all Asia and the world worships."

28 When they heard this they were filled with wrath and cried out, saying, "Great is Diana of Ephesus."

29 Then the city was filled with the confusion, and they rushed with one accord into the theater, having seized Gaius and Aristarchus, men of Macedonia, Paul's traveling companions.

30 When Paul was determined to enter into the theater, the disciples would not allow him.

31 Also certain friends of his from Asia sent to him and entreated him not to go into the theater.

32 Some there were crying one thing, and some another, for the assembly was in confusion, and most did not even know for what reason they had come together.

33 They brought Alexander out before the multitude as the Jews put him forward. So Alexander beckoned with his hand for silence so that he could make a defense to the people.

34 When they perceived that he was a Jew, all with one voice cried out for two hours, "Great is Diana of the Ephesians."

35 When the town clerk had quieted the multitude, he said, "You men of Ephesus, what man is there who does not know that the

city of the Ephesians is temple-keeper of the great Diana and of the image which fell down from heaven?

36 "Seeing then that these things cannot be disputed, you should be quiet, and do nothing rash.

37 "For you have brought these men here who are neither robbers of temples nor blasphemers of our goddess.

38 "If therefore Demetrius and the craftsmen who are with him have a matter against any man, the courts are open, and there are proconsuls; let them accuse one another there.

39 "If this is about other matters, it should be settled in the regular assembly.

40 "For indeed we are in danger of being accused of causing a riot concerning this, and since there is no cause for it, we will not be able to give an excuse for this."

41 When he had said this he dismissed the assembly.

The Holy Spirit at Ephesus

Acts 19:1-8: The disciples at Ephesus were obviously faithful men, but it was tragic that they only knew of the baptism of John. They were still stuck at the message that was to prepare the way for the One who was to come, but having not yet been led to Him who had already come. In this same way, many still get stuck in a message that is intended to prepare the way for something greater, but never move on to the greater. Even so, this is also encouragement not to give up on such as these who remain faithful to the level of truth that they have.

The School of Tyrannus

19:9-12: Paul taught two years in this school and the result was "all Asia heard the word of the Lord." How awesome must this class have been! Likewise, every Bible and theological school has potential to have great impact far beyond its walls when there is a sincere devotion to the truth.

The Jewish Exorcists

19:13-22: As this example with these Jewish exorcists shows, we only have true spiritual authority when the King lives in us. It is not enough to just know the name of the Lord or those who know the Lord—we must know Him ourselves.

Riots for Diana

19:23-41: The real issue that brought about this persecution was not truth, and not really about Diana, but it was about money. As discussed previously, this is the actual root of many persecutions and controversies throughout history.

NOTES

THE BOOK OF
ACTS
Acts 20

Paul Returns to Macedonia

1 After the uproar had ceased, Paul sent for the disciples and exhorted them. He then took leave of them and departed to go into Macedonia.

2 When he had gone through those parts and had given them much exhortation, he came into Greece.

3 There he spent three months, until a plot was made against him by the Jews as he was about to set sail for Syria, so he determined to return through Macedonia.

4 Some accompanied him as far as Asia, Sopater of Berea, the son of Pyrrhus; and of the Thessalonians, Aristarchus and Secundus; and Gaius of Derbe, Timothy, and from Asia, Tychicus and Trophimus.

5 These had gone before, and were waiting for us at Troas.

6 We sailed away from Philippi after the days of unleavened bread, and came to them at Troas in five days, where we tarried for seven days.

A Resurrection at Troas

7 On the first day of the week, when we were gathered together to break bread, Paul began to preach. As he was intending to depart on the next day, he prolonged his message until midnight.

8 There were many lights in the upper chamber where we were gathered together.

9 A young man named Eutychus sat in the window, and he fell asleep as Paul continued to speak, and he fell down from the third story, and was picked up dead.

10 Paul went down and fell on him and after embracing him, he said, "Do not be concerned; his life is in him." Then the boy arose.

11 When he had gone back up and had eaten, he continued to talk to them until daybreak, and then he departed.

12 So they brought the lad alive and were very comforted.

13 We were going before to the ship that set sail for Assos, and were there intending to take on Paul, but he decided to go by land.

14 When he met us at Assos, we took him on board and came to Mitylene.

15 Sailing from there we came the following day over to Chios, and the next day we came to Samos, and the day after we came to Miletus.

16 For Paul had determined to sail past Ephesus so that he would not have to spend time in Asia, because he was in a hurry to be in Jerusalem on the day of Pentecost if possible.

Paul's Farewell to Ephesus

17 From Miletus he sent to Ephesus and called to himself the elders of the church.

18 When they had come to him, he said to them, "You yourselves know that from the first day I set foot in Asia, the manner in which I lived was consistent,

19 "serving the Lord with humility, with tears, and with the trials which befell me from the plots of the Jews.

20 "Yet, I did not refrain from declaring to you anything that was profitable, and teaching you publicly, and from house to house,

21 "testifying both to Jews and to Greeks, repentance toward God and faith toward our Lord Jesus Christ.

22 "Now, I go bound in the spirit to Jerusalem, not knowing the things that will befall me there,

23 "except that the Holy Spirit testifies to me in every city, saying that bonds and afflictions await me.

24 "I do not count my life as dear to myself, so that I may accomplish my purpose, and the ministry which I received from the Lord Jesus to testify of the gospel of the grace of God.

25 "Now, I know that you all, among whom I went about preaching the kingdom, will not see my face again.

26 "Therefore, I testify to you this day, that I am innocent of the blood of all men,

27 "because I did not hold back from declaring to you the whole counsel of God.

28 "Take heed to yourselves, and to all the flock over which the Holy Spirit has made you overseers, to feed the church of the Lord that He purchased with His own blood.

29 "I know that after my departure grievous wolves will enter in among you, not sparing the flock,

30 "and from among your own number men will arise, speaking perverse things, to draw away the disciples after them.

31 "Therefore keep watch, remembering that for three years I did not cease to admonish every one night and day with tears.

32 "Now I commend you to God and to the word of His grace, that is able to build you up, and to give you the inheritance among all of those who are sanctified.

33 "I did not covet any man's silver, or gold, or apparel.

34 "You yourselves know that these hands ministered to my needs and to those who were with me.

35 "In all things I was an example to you, so that in your labors you should help the weak, and to remember the words of the Lord Jesus, that He Himself said, 'It is more blessed to give than to receive.'"

36 When he had finished speaking, he kneeled down and prayed with them all.

37 Then they all wept deeply and fell on Paul's neck and kissed him,

38 having great sorrow mostly because of his word that they would not see him again. So they stayed with him all the way to the ship.

Paul Returns to Macedonia

Acts 20:1-6: This chapter reveals the typical pattern of the apostolic team in their travels. Persecution, or a rejection

of the gospel, in a place would keep them moving. Where there was openness to the gospel, they would stay for a time to form the new believers into a church and help them get established.

A Resurrection at Troas

20:7-16: Here Paul has the distinction of preaching possibly the longest sermon in Scripture. There are many preachers who have caused people to fall asleep, but not many who have caused them to fall to their death! Neither are there many who could raise them from the dead if this happened.

Paul's Farewell to Ephesus

20:17-38: Paul's last speech to the elders of Ephesus is one of the great descriptions of his message and his lifestyle as an apostle. He fulfilled The Great Commission by teaching the "whole council of God." Paul lived a life of integrity and the highest standards of character so that there would be no reproach to the gospel.

Even though the scandals of preachers are constantly paraded in the headlines in our times, most preachers and most missionaries follow the example of this great apostle—preaching and standing for truth, and living lives of moderation that reflect their message. Let us always be thankful for such as these true servants of Christ.

NOTES

THE BOOK OF
ACTS
Acts 21

Paul Returns to Jerusalem

1 After we had parted from them and had set sail, we went on a straight course to Cos, and the next day to Rhodes, and from there to Patara.

2 Then we found a ship crossing over to Phoenicia, so we boarded it and set sail.

3 When we had come within sight of Cyprus, leaving it on the left hand, we sailed to Syria, and landed at Tyre, because there the ship was to unload its cargo.

4 There Paul found the disciples, so we tarried there for seven days. These said to Paul through the Spirit that he should not set foot in Jerusalem.

5 When we had accomplished our time there, we departed and continued on our journey, so they all, with wives and children, brought us on our way until we were out of the city. There, kneeling down on the beach, we prayed and said our farewells.

6 We went on board the ship, so they returned home.

7 When we had finished the voyage from Tyre, we arrived at Ptolemais. There we saluted the brethren and stayed with them for one day.

The Spirit Warns Paul

8 On the next day we departed and came to Caesarea; and entering into the house of Philip the evangelist, who was one of the seven, we stayed with him.

9   Now this man had four virgin daughters who prophesied.

10 As we tarried there for a few days, a prophet came down from Jerusalem named Agabus.

11 When he came to us, he took Paul's belt and bound his own feet and hands, and said, "Thus says the Holy Spirit, 'So will the Jews at Jerusalem bind the man who owns this belt, and will deliver him into the hands of the Gentiles.'"

12 When we heard these things, both those of us who were traveling with Paul, and those who were from that place, tried to persuade him not to go up to Jerusalem.

13 Then Paul answered, "What are you doing, weeping and breaking my heart? I am not only ready to be bound, but also to die at Jerusalem for the name of the Lord Jesus."

14 When he would not be persuaded, we stopped trying, saying, "The will of the Lord be done."

Paul Meets With the Elders

15 After these days we took up our baggage and went up to Jerusalem.

16 A disciple from Caesarea went with us, bringing with them one Mnason of Cyprus, an early disciple, with whom we would lodge.

17 When we had come to Jerusalem, the brethren received us gladly.

18 The following day Paul went with us to James, and all the elders were present.

19 When he had saluted them, he rehearsed one by one the things that God had wrought among the Gentiles through his ministry.

20 When they heard it, they glorified God, and then said to Paul, "You see, brother, how many thousands there are among the Jews of those who have believed and are all zealous for the Law.

21 "They have been informed concerning you, that you teach all the Jews who are among the Gentiles to forsake Moses, telling them not to circumcise their children, neither to walk after the traditions.

22 "It is certain that they will hear that you have come.

23 "Therefore, do this: We have four men who have made a vow.

24 "Take them and purify yourself with them, and pay their expenses so that they may shave their heads. Then all will know that there is no truth in the things that they have been told about you, but that you yourself also walk orderly, keeping the Law.

25 "Even so, concerning the Gentiles who have believed, we wrote giving the judgment that they should keep themselves from things sacrificed to idols, and from blood, and from what is strangled, and from fornication."

26 Then Paul took the men, and the next day purifying himself with them, he went into the temple, declaring the fulfillment of the days of purification until the offering was made for each of them.

Paul Stirs Jerusalem

27 When the seven days were almost completed, the Jews from Asia saw Paul in the temple and seized him, stirring up the multitude by crying out,

28 "Men of Israel, help! This is the man who teaches all men everywhere against the people, and the Law, and this place. Even worse than that, he also brought Greeks into the temple and has defiled this holy place."

29 For they had seen him before in the city with Trophimus the Ephesian, whom they assumed that Paul had brought into the temple.

30 So the whole city was stirred, and the people ran together, and they grabbed Paul, and dragged him out of the temple and immediately the doors were shut.

Paul Arrested

31 As they were seeking to kill him, news came to the commander of the Roman garrison that all of Jerusalem was in confusion.

32 So he quickly took soldiers and centurions and ran down into the crowd. When the people saw the commander and the soldiers, they stopped beating Paul.

33 Then the commander came and seized him, giving orders that he should be bound with chains. Then he inquired as to who he was and what he had done.

34 Some in the crowd shouted one thing, some another. When he could not understand the reason for the uproar, he commanded that Paul be brought into the fortress.

35 As Paul was being carried up the stairs by the soldiers because of the violence of the crowd,

36 the multitude continued to follow, crying out, "Away with him!"

37 So when Paul was about to be brought into the fortress, he said to the commander, "May I say something to you?" He replied, "Do you know Greek?"

38 "Are you not the Egyptian who recently stirred up sedition and led out into the wilderness the four thousand men of the Assassins?"

39 Paul answered, "I am a Jew of Tarsus in Cilicia, a citizen of no small city. I beseech you to give me a chance to speak to the people."

40 When he had given him permission, Paul, standing on the stairs, beckoned with his hand for the people to listen. Then a great silence came when he spoke to them in the Hebrew language.

Paul Returns to Jerusalem

Acts 21:1-7: Just as it seemed Paul never missed an opportunity to preach the gospel to win the lost, here we see that he also took every opportunity to strengthen the believers when he came across them.

The Spirit Warns Paul

21:8-14: Here we see that a warning about impending troubles does not always mean that we should try to avoid them, but the warnings are to help us prepare for them and the opportunity for the gospel that they are.

Paul Meets With the Elders

21:15-26: The persecution of Paul was because of his stand on the atonement of the cross that had supplanted the Law

as the basis of our righteousness. This same conflict continues to this day.

Paul Stirs Jerusalem

21:27-30: As is usually the case with those who stir up controversy, they will exaggerate or embellish perceived offenses because those who do this are serving the "father of lies."

Paul Arrested

21:31-40: The warnings Paul had received came to pass, and Paul, with all of the passion of an evangelist, seizes the opportunity to share the gospel with the multitude. That is a true apostolic heart.

NOTES

THE BOOK OF
ACTS
Acts 22

Paul's Testifies at Jerusalem

1 "Brethren and fathers, hear the defense that I now make to you."

2 When they heard him speak in the Hebrew language, they became even more quiet, so he continued,

3 "I am a Jew, born in Tarsus of Cilicia, but brought up in this city at the feet of Gamaliel, instructed according to the most strict devotion to the law of our fathers, being zealous for God, even as you all are this day.

4 "I persecuted this Way to the death, binding and delivering into prisons both men and women.

5 "To this fact the high priest and the elders can bear witness. From them I received letters concerning the brethren, and journeyed to Damascus to bring those who were there to Jerusalem in bonds to be punished.

6 "Then it came to pass, that as I made my journey, and drew near to Damascus at about noon, suddenly a great light from heaven shone all about me.

7 "I fell to the ground and heard a voice saying to me, 'Saul, Saul, why are you persecuting Me?'

8 "I answered, 'Who are You, Lord?' He said to me, 'I am Jesus of Nazareth, whom you are persecuting.'

9 "They who were with me beheld the light, but they did not hear the voice of Him that spoke to me.

10 "So I said, 'What should I do, Lord?' The Lord said to me, 'Arise

and go into Damascus, and there it will be told to you all of the things that are appointed for you to do.'

11 "I could not see because the glory of that light had blinded me, so I was led to Damascus by the hand of those who were with me.

12 "Then one Ananias, a devout man according to the Law, who was of a good reputation with all the Jews who dwelt there,

13 "came to me, and standing next to me said, 'Brother Saul, receive your sight.' At that very moment I looked up at him.

14 "Then he said, 'The God of our fathers has appointed you to know His will, and to see the Righteous One, and to hear His voice.

15 'You will be a witness for Him to all men of what you have seen and heard.

16 'Now, why do you wait? Arise and be baptized, and wash away your sins, calling on His name.'

17 "So it came to pass that when I had returned to Jerusalem, and while I prayed in the temple, I fell into a trance,

18 "and saw Him saying to me, 'Hurry, and get out of Jerusalem quickly, because they will not receive your testimony concerning Me.'

19 "So I said, 'Lord, they themselves know that I imprisoned and beat those in every synagogue that believed in You:

20 'and when the blood of Stephen Your witness was shed, I was standing by, consenting, and keeping the garments of those who killed him.'

21 "So He said to me, 'Depart, for I will send you far away from here to the Gentiles.'"

Jerusalem Rejects Paul's Testimony

22 The people listened to his word up to this point, and then they cried out, saying, "Away with such a fellow from the earth–for he is not fit to live."

23 As they cried out they threw off their garments and cast dust into the air,

24 so the commander ordered him to be brought into the fortress,

saying that he should be examined by scourging so that he might know for what cause they were so enraged against him.

25 When they had tied him up with the thongs, Paul said to the centurion that stood by, "Is it lawful for you to scourge a man who is a Roman and has not been condemned?"

26 When the centurion heard it, he went to the commander and said, "What are you about to do? For this man is a Roman."

27 The commander came and said to him, "Tell me, are you a Roman?" He answered, "Yes."

28 The commander then said, "It cost me a great sum of money to obtain my citizenship." Paul replied, "But I was born a Roman."

29 So those who were about to examine him immediately drew back, and the commander was also afraid when he learned that he was a Roman, because he had bound him.

30 On the next day, desiring to know for certain why he was accused by the Jews, he loosed him, and commanded the chief priests and all the council to come together, and brought Paul down and set him before them.

Paul's Testifies at Jerusalem

Acts 22:1-21: Beginnings are important. Paul reveals here how the power of his first encounter with the Lord guided the rest of his life. Do we remember how He first touched us and set the course of our lives? Have we stayed on that course?

This is also another example of how Paul used every occasion to preach the gospel. How can we not help but to do the same?

Jerusalem Rejects Paul's Testimony

22:22-30: It is interesting that it was when Paul said that he had been sent to the Gentiles that the people refused to hear anymore. The divide between Jew and Gentile remains one of the strongest racial barriers, but it is one that the Lord promises He will remove through His church when Jew and Gentile become "one new man" (see Ephesians 2:15).

We see here that Paul was not hesitant to use his Roman citizenship to avoid being beaten when he had not brought it up at other times to avoid persecution. From this point on, Paul was turning to the authority of the Roman Empire, which would lead to his trial before Caesar. This was obviously the will of the Lord so that Paul could witness to Caesar.

NOTES

THE BOOK OF
ACTS
Acts 23

Paul's Testimony Before the Council

1 So Paul looked steadfastly at the council and said, "Brethren, I have lived before God with a good conscience until this day."

2 The high priest Ananias then commanded those who stood by him to strike him on the mouth.

3 Then Paul said to him, "God will strike you, you whitewashed wall. Do you sit to judge me according to the Law, and command me to be struck contrary to the Law?"

4 The ones who stood by him said, "Do you revile God's high priest?"

5 Paul said, "Brethren, I did not know that he was the high priest: for it is written, **'You shall not speak evil of a ruler of your people'** (Exodus 22:8).

6 When Paul perceived that one part of the council were Sadducees and the other Pharisees, he cried out, "Brethren, I am a Pharisee, a son of Pharisees. It is for my hope in the resurrection of the dead that I am being judged."

7 When he said this, there arose a dissension between the Pharisees and Sadducees, and the assembly was divided.

8 For the Sadducees say that there is no resurrection, nor angel, or spirit, but the Pharisees acknowledge them all.

9 So there arose a great clamor, and some of the scribes of the Pharisees stood up and contended, saying, "We find no evil in this man. What if a spirit or an angel has spoken to him?"

10 Soon the dissension became so great that the commander became afraid that Paul would be torn to pieces by them, so he commanded

the soldiers to go down and take him by force from their midst, and bring him into the fortress.

11 The night following the Lord stood next to Paul, and said, "Be of good cheer, for just as you have testified concerning Me at Jerusalem, so you must bear witness also at Rome."

The Plot to Kill Paul

12 On the next day, some of the Jews banded together and bound themselves under a curse, saying that they would neither eat nor drink until they had killed Paul.

13 There were more than forty that made this conspiracy.

14 So they came to the chief priests and the elders, and said, "We have bound ourselves under a curse to taste nothing until we have killed Paul.

15 "Therefore do this: Have the council ask the commander to bring him down to you as though you would examine his case more thoroughly, and we will be ready to slay him when he comes near."

16 However, Paul's nephew heard of their plot, and he entered into the fortress and told Paul.

17 Paul then called one of the centurions and said, "Bring this young man to the commander; he has something to tell him."

18 So he brought him to the commander and said, "Paul the prisoner called me and asked me to bring this young man to you who has something to tell you."

19 The commander took him by the hand and drew him aside, asking him privately, "What is it that you want to tell me?"

20 He said, "The Jews have agreed to ask you to bring Paul down to the council tomorrow, as though they would inquire somewhat more thoroughly concerning him.

21 "Do not yield to them, because there will be about forty men lying in wait for him who have bound themselves under a curse to neither eat nor to drink until they have slain him. They are ready now and are just looking for the promise from you."

22 So the commander let the young man go, charging him, "Tell no one that you have told me these things."

Paul Is Sent to Felix

23 The commander then called two of the centurions and said, "Get two hundred soldiers with spears to go as far as Caesarea, along with seventy horsemen, and be ready to go at 9:00 p.m."

24 He also told them to provide a beast for Paul to sit on and to bring him safely to Felix the governor.

25 Then he wrote a letter to go with Paul, saying:

26 "Claudius Lysias to the most excellent governor Felix, greetings.

27 "This man was seized by the Jews and was about to be slain by them when I came upon them with soldiers and rescued him, having learned that he was a Roman.

28 "And desiring to know the cause for which they accused him, I brought him down to their council.

29 "I found that he was being accused about questions concerning their Law, but there is nothing in the charges worthy of death or prison.

30 "When it was revealed to me that there was a plot against the man, I sent him to you right away, charging his accusers also to bring their charges against him before you."

31 So the soldiers took Paul just as it was commanded them and brought him by night to Antipatris.

32 On the next day, they left the horsemen to go with him and returned to the fortress.

33 When they came to Caesarea and delivered the letter to the governor, they presented Paul before him.

34 When he had read it, he asked what province he was from, and when he understood that he was from Cilicia,

35 he said, "I will hear you fully when your accusers have also come." So he commanded him to be kept in Herod's palace.

Paul's Testimony Before the Council

Acts 23:1-11: Paul later confessed that his crying out that he was on trial for the hope in the resurrection was wrong because he did it to cause dissention in the council. It was true that he was on trial for the hope of the gospel that in

Christ there will be a resurrection, but he should not have used this to cause dissension. Truth will not bring life unless it is used for the right purpose.

The Plot to Kill Paul

23:12-22: The Jewish system of justice was by far the most equitable in the world at the time and remains so today. For this council, which was the supreme court of the Jewish nation, to consent to be a part of such a conspiracy was a basic violation of the Law and of justice. The best system of justice will still be unjust if there are unjust people in it.

Paul Is Sent to Felix

23:23-35: We see here that every attack on Paul only resulted in his being able to testify of the Lord before more rulers, fulfilling his destiny that was told to him when he was converted.

NOTES

THE BOOK OF
ACTS
Acts 24

Paul's Accusers

1   After five days the high priest Ananias came down with some of the elders, and an orator named Tertullus, to testify to the governor against Paul.

2   When he was called, Tertullus began to accuse him, saying, "Seeing that by you we enjoy much peace, and that by your providence problems are being corrected for this nation,

3   "we accept it in all ways and in all places, most excellent Felix, with great appreciation.

4   "But, so that I do not become tedious to you, I entreat you to hear our brief argument.

5   "We have found this man a real pest, and a promoter of rebellion among all the Jews throughout the world, and a ringleader of the sect of the Nazarenes.

6   "He even tried to profane the temple, so that we arrested him. We would have judged him according to our Law,

7   "but the commander, Lysias, came, and with great violence took him away,

8   "commanding his accusers to come before you. From these you will be able, by examining him yourself, to verify all of these things of which we accuse him."

9   The Jews also joined in the charge, affirming that these things were so.

Paul's Defense

10 When the governor had beckoned him to speak, Paul answered, "For as much as I know that you have judged our nation for many years, I cheerfully make my defense.

11 "It has only been twelve days since I went up to worship at Jerusalem.

12 "Neither did they find me disputing with any man in the temple, nor stirring up a crowd, neither in the synagogues, nor in the city.

13 "Neither can they prove to you the things which they now accuse me of.

14 "But this I confess to you, that according to the Way which they call a sect, I do serve the God of our fathers, believing all things that are in the Law and in the Prophets,

15 "having hope toward God, which these men also have, that there shall be a resurrection both of the just and unjust.

16 "Because of this, I continually exercise myself to have a good conscience, void of offense toward God and men in every way.

17 "Now after some years I came to bring alms and offerings to my nation,

18 "which I was doing when they found me purified in the temple, with no crowd, nor with a disturbance, but there were certain Jews from Asia,

19 "who should have been here before you to make this accusation, if they had anything against me.

20 "Otherwise, let these men themselves say what wrongdoing they found when I stood before the council,

21 "except for this one statement that I cried out when standing among them, 'That it is because of the hope of the resurrection of the dead I am called in question before you this day.'"

22 So Felix, having knowledge concerning the Way, deferred to them, saying, "When Lysias the commander comes, I will determine your matter."

23 He then gave orders to the centurion that Paul should be kept in custody, but should be given liberties, and not to forbid any of his friends to minister to him.

Felix Challenged by the Gospel

24 After a few days, Felix came with Drusilla, his wife, who was a Jewess, and sent for Paul, and heard him concerning the faith in Christ Jesus.

25 As he spoke on righteousness, and self-control, and the judgment to come, great fear came upon Felix, and he said, "Go your way for now, and when I have a convenient time, I will call you again."

26 It was because he hoped that money would be given to him by Paul that he sent for him often and conversed with him.

27 When two years had passed, Felix was succeeded by Porcius Festus; and desiring to gain favor with the Jews, Felix left Paul in custody.

Paul's Accusers

Acts 24:1-9: For Ananias the high priest to come all the way to Caesarea with Paul's accusers reveals the high level of agitation that the leaders of Israel had with Paul and the Christians. Their agitation was focused on what they considered a disgrace to the temple, yet God Himself is never brought into the conversation by Paul's accusers. This reveals how they had come to esteem the temple of the Lord above the Lord of the temple, which is a basic diversion from true worship of God to worshiping the things of God.

Paul's Defense

24:10-23: In a brilliant defense, Paul simply refutes the accusations against him, and then uses the opportunity to testify of and defend the gospel of Christ, the defense of which Paul seems much more interested in making rather than defending himself. This is true faith.

Felix Challenged by the Gospel

24:24-27: Felix, the Roman Procurator, being interested in the gospel, sent for Paul to hear it with his wife. He obviously became convicted by the Holy Spirit when hearing of the

judgment to come. The judgment is coming, and the testimony of it does have great power of conviction, especially to those in leadership. This must be recovered as a part of the testimony of the gospel of the kingdom that must be preached before the end of this age can come.

NOTES

THE BOOK OF
ACTS
Acts 25

A Second Attempt to Kill Paul

1   Festus therefore, having come into the province, after three days went up to Jerusalem from Caesarea.

2   The chief priests and the principal men of the Jews informed him about Paul, and they entreated him,

3   asking a favor, that he would send him to Jerusalem, for which they laid a plot to kill him on the way.

4   However, Festus answered that Paul was to be kept in custody at Caesarea and that he himself was about to depart for it shortly, saying,

5   "Let those who are with authority among you go down with me, and if there is anything wrong with this man, let them accuse him."

6   When he had tarried among them for not more than nine or ten days, he went down to Caesarea. On the next day he sat on the judgment seat, and commanded Paul to be brought.

7   When he had come, the Jews who had come down from Jerusalem stood around him, bringing many grievous charges against him that they could not prove;

8   while Paul said in his defense, "Neither against the Law of the Jews, nor against the temple, nor against Caesar, have I transgressed in any way."

9   Festus, desiring to gain favor with the Jews, answered Paul and said, "Will you go up to Jerusalem and there be judged on these things before me?"

Paul Appeals to Caesar

10 Paul replied, "I will stand before Caesar's judgment seat, where I should be judged. To the Jews I have done no wrong, as you very well know.

11 "If I was a wrongdoer, or had I committed anything worthy of death, I would not refuse to die. But if none of those things are true of which these accuse me, no man can give me up to them. I appeal to Caesar."

12 Then Festus, when he had conferred with the council, answered, "You have appealed to Caesar, so to Caesar you shall go."

13 Now when certain days had passed, Agrippa the King, and Bernice, arrived at Caesarea, to pay their respects to Festus.

14 As they tarried there many days, Festus laid Paul's case before the King, saying, "There is a certain man left a prisoner by Felix;

15 "about whom, when I was at Jerusalem, the chief priests and the elders of the Jews informed me, asking for a sentence against him.

16 "To whom I answered, that it is not the custom of the Romans to give up any man before the accused meets their accusers face to face and have had an opportunity to make his defense concerning the matter laid against him.

17 "When therefore they had come together here, I made no delay, but on the next day sat on the judgment seat, and commanded the man to be brought.

18 "Concerning whom, when the accusers stood up, they brought no charge of such evil things as I expected,

19 "but had certain grievances against him concerning their own religion, and of one Jesus, who was dead, but whom Paul affirmed to be alive.

20 "Being perplexed about how to inquire concerning these things, I asked whether he would go to Jerusalem and there be judged on these matters.

21 "When Paul had appealed to be kept for the decision of the emperor, I commanded him to be kept until I could send him to Caesar."

22 Agrippa said to Festus, "I also would like to hear the man myself." So he said, "Tomorrow you will hear him."

23 On the next day, when Agrippa had come and Bernice with great pomp, and they had entered into the place of the hearing with the chief captains and principal men of the city, at the command of Festus, Paul was brought in.

24 Festus said, "King Agrippa, and all men who are here present with us, you behold this man, about whom all the multitude of the Jews made suit to me, both at Jerusalem and here, declaring that he should not live any longer.

25 "But I found that he had committed nothing worthy of death, but as he himself appealed to the emperor, I determined to send him.

26 "But of this matter I have no clear account to write to my lord. Therefore I have brought him before you, King Agrippa, so that after this examination I may have something to write.

27 "For it seems unreasonable to me to send a prisoner and not to signify the charges against him."

Second Plot to Kill Paul

Acts 25:1-9: As is often the case with persecutions against those who preach the gospel, the accusations are trumped up charges with no basis. However, the challenge of the gospel is so grievous to those who do evil that if they cannot win by perverting the system of justice, they will often resort to murder, as they tried to do with Paul. Whether martyrdom is the result of an official state decree against Christians, or murder, it is usually the mark of an uncompromising devotion to Christ, who was Himself the most unjustly condemned Man to ever walk the earth.

Paul Appeals to Caesar

Acts 25:10-27: It may seem a waste for the great apostle to have been kept in prison for all of this time, but what he was able to do because of this was write many of the Epistles that are now canon Scripture. Through these letters, he has

accomplished more throughout the church age than any amount of his missionary labors could have done.

Many Christians wrestle with whether they should ever sue. Here we have a biblical precedent with Paul suing Israel by appealing to Caesar. This does not mean that suing others is the right thing to do, especially when we are taking a brother or sister before the heathen as Paul warned the Corinthians about doing, but it can be necessary as it was here with Paul.

NOTES

THE BOOK OF
ACTS
Acts 26

Paul's Testimony Before Agrippa and Festus

1 Agrippa said to Paul, "You are permitted to speak for yourself." Then Paul stretched forth his hand and made his defense:

2 "I consider myself fortunate, king Agrippa, to make my defense before you today about all the things I am accused of by the Jews,

3 "especially since you are an expert in the customs and questions concerning the Jews. Therefore I beseech you to hear me patiently.

4 "My manner of life from my youth up, which was from the beginning among my own nation and at Jerusalem, is known by all the Jews.

5 "Having knowledge of me from the first, if they are willing to testify, that after the strictest sect of our religion I lived as a Pharisee.

6 "Now I stand here to be judged for the hope of the promise made by God to our fathers;

7 "to which promise our twelve tribes, earnestly serving God night and day, hope to attain. It is for this hope that I am accused by the Jews, O King.

8 "Why is it judged incredible to you, if God does raise the dead?

9 "I thought this myself, but felt that I should do many things against the name of Jesus of Nazareth.

10 "So this I did in Jerusalem, imprisoning many of the saints for which I received authority from the chief priests. When they were put to death, I gave my vote against them.

11 "Pursuing and punishing them continually in all the synagogues,

I strove to make them blaspheme, and being exceedingly enraged against them, I persecuted them even to foreign cities.

12 "It was as I was engaged in this way that I journeyed to Damascus with the authority and commission of the chief priests,

13 "and at midday, O King, I saw on the way a light from heaven, more bright than the sun, shining all around me and those who journeyed with me.

14 "When we had all fallen to the ground, I heard a voice saying to me in the Hebrew language, 'Saul, Saul, why are you persecuting Me? Is it hard for you to kick against the goads?'

15 "I replied, 'Who are You, Lord?' Then the Lord said, 'I am Jesus whom you are persecuting.

16 'Now arise, and stand upon your feet. For this reason I have appeared to you, to appoint you a minister and a witness both of the things which you have now seen of Me and of the things in which I will appear to you;

17 'delivering you from this people and from the Gentiles, to whom I will send you,

18 'to open their eyes so that they may turn from darkness to light, and from the power of Satan to God, so that they may receive remission of sins and an inheritance among those who are sanctified by faith in Me.'

19 "Therefore, O King Agrippa, I was not disobedient to the heavenly vision,

20 "but declared first to those in Damascus, and then at Jerusalem, and throughout all the country of Judea, and also to the Gentiles, that they should repent and turn to God, doing works worthy of repentance.

21 "For this cause the Jews seized me in the temple and tried to kill me.

22 "Having therefore obtained help from God, I stand to this day testifying both to small and great, saying nothing but what the Prophets and Moses all said would come to pass;

23 "how the Christ must suffer, and how that He, first by the resurrection of the dead, should proclaim light both to these people and to the Gentiles."

24 As Paul made his defense, Festus said with a loud voice, "Paul, you are mad! Your great learning has made you go mad."

25 Paul replied, "I am not mad, most excellent Festus, but speak words of sober truth.

26 "For the king knows of these things of which I speak freely, for I am persuaded that none of these things are hidden from him, because none of this was done in a corner.

27 "King Agrippa, do you believe the Prophets? I know that you believe them."

28 Agrippa then said to Paul, "With but a little persuasion you would try to make me a Christian."

29 Paul replied, "I would to God, that whether with little or with much, not only you, but also all that hear me this day, might become such as I am, except for these bonds."

30 The king then stood up with the governor and Bernice who had sat together,

31 and when they had withdrawn, they spoke to one another, saying, "This man did nothing worthy of death or even bonds."

32 Agrippa said to Festus, "This man might have been set free if he had not appealed to Caesar."

Paul's Testimony Before Agrippa and Festus

Acts 26:1-32: This testimony of Paul was powerful because it was well-known by the Jews about his former life as a Pharisee and as a ruthless persecutor of Christians. Then he suddenly becomes one of the chief advocates of the message of Jesus Christ. No doubt many dismissed this as Paul having just gone mad, which Agrippa here tries to assert, but Paul himself was a man of such clarity and soberness of spirit that this charge was easily refuted. Even so, it is not recorded that Agrippa converted, but he at least did not persecute the church as his father had done. We cannot always know the purpose of our witness, but we can be sure that the word of the Lord will accomplish its purpose.

Verse 14: When the Lord asked Paul if it was hard to kick against the goads, this is in reference to the grate around the altar of burnt offering. The sacrificial animals used to kick against this before being sacrificed. Paul, an expert in the Law, would have known right away what this meant—that his life was about to become a sacrifice.

NOTES

THE BOOK OF
ACTS
Acts 27

Paul Sails for Rome

1 When it was determined that we should sail for Italy, they delivered Paul and the other prisoners to a centurion named Julius of the Augustan band.

2 We embarked on a ship of Adramyttium, which was about to sail to the places on the coast of Asia. So we put to sea, Aristarchus, a Macedonian of Thessalonica, being with us.

3 The next day we stopped at Sidon, and Julius treated Paul kindly and gave him leave to go to his friends and refresh himself.

4 Putting to sea from there, we sailed under the lee of Cyprus, because the winds were contrary.

5 When we had sailed across the sea which is off Cilicia and Pamphylia, we came to Myra, a city of Lycia.

6 There the centurion found a ship of Alexandria sailing for Italy, and he put us on it.

7 When we had sailed slowly many days and were making progress with difficulty toward Cnidus with the wind against us, we sailed under the lee of Crete, opposite Salmone.

8 With difficulty, we were coasting along it and came to a place called Fair Havens, which was close to the city of Lasea.

Paul's Warns the Centurion

9 After we had spent a lot of time there and the voyage was now dangerous, because the Fast had already passed, Paul admonished them,

10 and said, "Gentlemen, I perceive that the voyage will be with injury and much loss, not only of the lading and the ship, but also of our lives."

11 However, the centurion gave more heed to the ship's master, who was also the owner of the ship, than to what was said by Paul.

12 Because the port was not adequate to spend the winter in, most accepted the advice to put to sea from there if by any means we could reach Phoenix and winter there, which is a port of Crete that runs northeast and southeast.

13 When the south wind blew softly, supposing that they had obtained their purpose, they weighed anchor and sailed along Crete close to shore.

The Storm

14 After a short time there came upon us a tempestuous wind, which is called Euraquilo.

15 When the ship was caught and could not face the wind, we gave way to it and were driven along by it.

16 Running under the lee of a small island called Clauda, we were able to secure the boat only with great difficulty.

17 When they had hoisted it up, they used supports to undergird the ship, and fearing that they should be cast upon the Syrtis, which are the shifting sands off the coast, they lowered the sails and ropes and so we were driven along.

18 As we labored exceedingly against the storm, the next day they began to throw the freight overboard.

19 The third day they cast the tackling of the ship out with their own hands.

20 When neither sun nor stars appeared for many days, and no small tempest continued, all hope that we would be saved was lost.

Angelic Encouragement

21 When they had gone a long time without food, Paul stood up in their midst and said, "Gentlemen, you should have listened to me

and not have set sail from Crete so that we would not have suffered this damage and loss.

22 "Even so, now I exhort you to be of good cheer. There will be no loss of life among you, but only of the ship.

23 "For there stood by me this night an angel of the God to whom I belong and whom I serve,

24 "saying, 'Fear not, Paul, you must stand before Caesar, and God has granted you all who sail with you.'

25 "Therefore, be of good cheer, for I believe God and know that it will be even so as it has been told to me.

26 "However, we must be cast upon a certain island."

27 When the fourteenth night had come, as we were driven back and forth in the sea of Adria, about midnight the sailors observed that we were drawing near to land.

28 When they sounded, it was twenty fathoms. After a short time, they sounded again and found it to be fifteen fathoms.

29 Fearing that we should be cast ashore on rocky ground, they let out four anchors from the stern and hoped for the light of day.

30 As the sailors were seeking to flee the ship secretly, and had lowered the boat into the sea, under the pretense that they would lay out anchors from the bow of the ship,

31 Paul said to the centurion and to the soldiers, "Except these stay in the ship, you cannot be saved."

32 Then the soldiers cut away the ropes of the boat and let her fall off.

33 While the day was coming, Paul encouraged them all to take some food, saying, "This day is the fourteenth day that you wait and continue fasting, having taken nothing.

34 "Therefore I beseech you to take some food. This is for your wellbeing, for there will not a hair perish from the head of any of you."

35 When he had said this and had taken bread, he gave thanks to God in the presence of all, and he broke it and began to eat.

36 Then they were all of good cheer, and they also took food.

37 There were on the ship two hundred seventy-six souls.

38 When they had eaten enough, they lightened the ship, throwing out the wheat into the sea.

39 When the day broke, they did not recognize the land, but they perceived a certain bay with a beach, and they took counsel whether they could drive the ship upon it.

40 Then they cast off the anchors, and at the same time, loosening the bands of the rudders and hoisting up the foresail to the wind, they made for the beach.

41 Coming upon a place where two seas met, they ran the vessel aground, and the bow struck and remained unmovable, but the stern began to break up by the violence of the waves.

42 So the soldiers' counsel was to kill the prisoners, so that none of them should swim away and escape.

43 However, the centurion wanted to save Paul, and so kept them from their purpose. He then commanded that those who could swim should cast themselves overboard and get to the land first,

44 and the rest left the ship, some on planks, and some on other things from the ship. So it came to pass that they all escaped safely to the land.

Paul Sails for Rome

Acts 27:1-8: This indicates the difficulty of sea travel in those times. They had to find one ship after another that was going in the right direction until they finally reached their destination.

Paul's Warns the Centurion

27:9-13: These five verses reveal the most common elements that put people in jeopardy of a shipwreck, whether it is of their faith, their marriage, their profession, business, or mission:

    1) Failure to discern and heed the warning of the Lord.

    2) Impatience—they were in a hurry to get to Rome. The fruit of the Spirit is patience, so if we are allowing

impatience to control us, we will not be led by the Spirit, and the outcome will usually be bad.

3) Dissatisfaction with their circumstances—they did not feel that the port that they were in was adequate. The combination of impatience and dissatisfaction is deadly.

4) The above three set them up to fall prey to the trap of seemingly favorable circumstances to do what the above was driving them to do. Nowhere in Scripture are we taught to be guided by circumstances, but rather by the Spirit.

The French Bible translates verse 13 "supposing that they were masters of their own destiny." which may be more accurate, and certainly the cause of many a shipwreck.

The Storm

27:14-20: Above they supposed that they were "masters of their destiny," but here the crew of this ship made the additional mistake of letting the storm take control of their destiny and drive them along. Many Christians do the same, letting circumstances dictate their course and by this think they are submitting to God, but are in fact submitting to circumstances they are called to overcome. There is a reason why the faithful ones in the Book of Revelation are called "overcomers." We are not to be led by circumstances, but by God, which will often have us in opposition to circumstances.

Angelic Encouragement

27:21-44: Paul had a destiny in Rome so there was no way that he would be lost. The angel reminds him of this, and because of his destiny, Paul was not just a passenger with them, but the angel asserts that the passengers and crew would all be saved because they were with him. The purpose and destiny of God will trump any obstacles or threats that will seek to stop us.

NOTES

The Book of
ACTS
Acts 28

Malta

1 When we had escaped, we learned that the island was called Malta.

2 The natives showed us great kindness as they kindled a fire and received us all because of the rain and cold.

3 When Paul was gathering a bundle of sticks and laid them on the fire, a viper came out because of the heat and fastened onto his hand.

4 When the natives saw the venomous creature hanging from his hand, they said to one another, "No doubt this man is a murderer, so that even though he has escaped from the sea, yet justice has not permitted him to live."

5 However, he shook off the creature into the fire and was not harmed.

6 They kept waiting for him to swell up or fall down suddenly and die, but after a long time passed and nothing happened to him, they changed their minds and said that he was a god.

7 Now in the neighborhood of that place were lands belonging to the chief man of the island, named Publius, who received us and entertained us courteously for three days.

All Are Healed

8 As the father of Publius lay sick of fever and dysentery, Paul went to him and prayed, laying his hands on him, and healed him.

9 When this was done, the rest also that had diseases on the island came and were healed.

10 Then they gave us many honors, and when we sailed, they gave us all that we needed.

11 So after three months, we set sail in a ship of Alexandria which had wintered on the island, whose sign was The Twin Brothers.

12 As we came to port at Syracuse, we stayed there for three days.

13 From there we made a circuit and arrived at Rhegium, and after one day a south wind sprang up, and on the second day we came to Puteoli,

14 where we found brethren who and entreated us to stay with them for seven days, and so we came to Rome.

Rome

15 From there the brethren, when they heard of us, came to meet us as far as The Market of Appius and The Three Taverns. When Paul saw them, he thanked God and took courage.

16 When we entered into Rome, Paul was allowed to stay by himself with the soldier that guarded him.

17 So it came to pass that after three days he called together those who were the leaders of the Jews, and when they had come together, he said to them, "Brethren, I have done nothing against our people or the customs of our fathers, yet was delivered as a prisoner in Jerusalem into the hands of the Romans,

18 "who, when they had examined me, desired to set me free, because there was no cause of death in me.

19 "When the Jews protested, I was compelled to appeal to Caesar, but not because I had an accusation against my nation.

20 "For this cause I entreat you to listen to me because it is for the hope of Israel I am bound with this chain."

21 So they said to him, "We neither received letters from Judea concerning you, nor did any of the brethren who have come here report or speak anything bad about you.

22 "But we desire to hear from you what you think, because, concerning this sect, it is known to us that everywhere it is spoken against."

23 When they had appointed him a day they came to him at his lodging in great numbers. So he expounded and testified concerning the kingdom of God, and was persuading them concerning Jesus from both the Law of Moses and the prophets, from morning until evening.

24 Some believed the things that were spoken, and some disbelieved.

25 When they could not agree among themselves, they departed after Paul had spoken one last exhortation, saying, "Well spoke the Holy Spirit through Isaiah the prophet to your fathers,

26 "saying, **'Go to this people, and say, "By hearing you may hear, but shall not understand. And seeing you may see, but shall not perceive.**

27 **"'For this people's hearts have become hard, their ears are dull of hearing, and they have closed their eyes; lest they should perceive with their eyes, hear with their ears, or understand with their heart, should turn again, and I should heal them'"** **(Isaiah 6:9-10).**

28 "Therefore let it be known to you that this salvation of God is sent to the Gentiles because they will listen."

29 When he had said these things, the Jews departed, disputing greatly among themselves.

30 So he stayed two whole years in his own hired dwelling and received all that came to him,

31 preaching the kingdom of God, and teaching the things concerning the Lord Jesus Christ with all boldness, and none were hindering him.

Malta

Acts 28:1-7: The tiny island of Malta later became one of the most strategic sites in the world in the clashes between Christian Europe and Islam. It endured one of the worst sieges of all-time when one of the massive armies of Suleiman the Magnificent invaded it, having a navy so large that it was said that the Mediterranean Sea looked like a forest because of the masts. After months of some of the most terrible and intense fighting of the Middle Ages, about three thousand Christian

knights and militia turned back the huge armies of Islam, and they never again seriously threatened Europe.

In World War II, the same little island endured the second worst bombing of any Allied city in the war after London. With only three old and outclassed fighter planes named "Faith," "Hope," and "Charity," all of which sacrificed themselves in the face of the overwhelming onslaught of the Nazi air force, the islanders never considered surrender. Their endurance helped turn the battle for North Africa in favor of the Allies and kept the Mediterranean Sea open for Allied shipping.

The obvious question is: How could such a small island (just fifteen miles square), play such a huge and strategic role in history? How could the same people, centuries apart, demonstrate such courage and endurance? They attribute it to living by the "faith, hope, and charity" that the author of those famous terms, Paul, obviously imparted to them while being hosted on this island. What an impact a seeming accident would have for nearly two thousand years! We must never consider that our trials are useless, even if we don't directly see the fruit of them. Even our shipwrecks that seem to us such disasters can bear more fruit than we can imagine as long as we stay on course to fulfill our purpose in God.

All Are Healed

28:8-14: Paul, ever the evangelist and missionary, constantly used his spiritual gifts to touch those he encountered. When he had a chance to visit and strengthen some of the brethren, he took the opportunity. Paul's trip to Rome was a trail of blessing and healing that ultimately impacted multitudes. The destination is important, but the journey can be too.

Rome

28:9-31: Paul spends two years waiting for his trial before Caesar, and spent it all preaching Jesus and teaching on the kingdom of God. He did this using "Moses and the Prophets," which were the only Scriptures they had at the time as the

New Testament had not yet been complied. What we call The Old Testament was far more than the Law, but as Jesus said of it, "the Law prophesied until John" (see Matthew 11:13). When we grasp how the Law was a prophecy, we begin to see that it is actually the deepest and most comprehensive revelation of both Jesus as the Christ and of the coming kingdom of God.

According to John Calvin, Paul's first coming to Rome was in the year 61. He was released and returned to Judea in 63, coming back to Rome in 65, when he was arrested and finished his course, being honored by the Lord with martyrdom.

NOTES

Book of Acts
Proper Names and Definitions

Aaron: a teacher, lofty, mountain of strength, fluent, light bearer

Abraham: father of a great multitude, exalted father

Achaia: grief, trouble

Adramyttium: the court of death

Aeneas: praised, praiseworthy

Agabus: a locust, the father's joy or feast

Agrippa: one who causes great pain at his birth

Alexander: one who assists men

Alphaeus: leader or chief

Amos: loading, weighty, burden bearer, strong

Ananias: or Ananiah, the cloud of the Lord

Andrew: a strong man, manly

Annas: one who answers, humble, merciful

Antioch: speedy as a chariot

Antipatris: for, or against the father

Apollonia: perdition, destruction

Apollos: one who destroys, destroyer

Aquila: an eagle

Arabians: native of Arabia

Areopagus: the hill of Mars

Aristarchus: the best prince

Asia: muddy, boggy

Assos: approaching, coming near

Attalia: that increases or sends

Azotus: effusion, inclination, theft

Babylon: confusion, also the gate of god, mixture

Barnabas: son of the prophet, or son of encouragement

Bartholomew: son of Tolmai, a son that suspends the waters

Benjamin: son of the right hand

Berea: heavy, weighty

Bernice: one that brings victory

Bithynia: violent precipitation

Blastus: that buds or brings forth

Caesar: title of Roman Emperors

Canaan: merchant, trader, or that humbles and subdues

Candace: who possesses contrition

Cappadocia: a sphere, buckle, or hand

Chios: open, opening

Christ: anointed

Cilicia: which rolls or overturns

Claudius: lame

Cnidus: age

Corinth: that which is satisfied, ornament, beauty

Cornelius: of a horn

Crete: carnal, fleshly

Crispus: curled

Cyprus: fair, fairness, Chittim islander; bruisers

Cyrene: a wall, coldness, the floor

Damaris: a little woman

Damascus: a sack full of blood, the similitude of burning, city of Syria, silent is the sackcloth weaver

David: well-beloved, dear

Demetrius: belonging to corn, or to Ceres

Derbe: a sting

Diana: luminous, perfect

Dionysius: divinely touched

Dorcas: a female doe—deer

Drusilla: watered by the dew

Egypt: the two lands, double straights, that troubles or oppresses, anguish

Egyptian: citizen of Egypt, the two lands

Egyptians: natives of Egypt, meaning the two lands

Elamites: natives of Elam

Elymas: a magician, a corrupter

Ephesus: desirable

Epicurean: follower of Epicurus, i.e., of one who gives assistance

Erastus: lovely, amiable

Ethiopia: blackness, heat, burned face

Ethiopians: Cushite, blackness, heat, burned face

Eutychus: happy, fortunate

Felix: happy, prosperous

Festus: festive, joyful

Gaius: lord, an earthly man

Galatia: white, the color of milk

Galilee: wheel, revolution, circle or circuit

Gallio: who sucks, or lives on milk

Gamaliel: recompense of God, camel of God

Gaza: a goat, stronghold

Gentiles: the nations or pagan

Greece: effervescent

Hamor: an ass, clay, dirt

Haran: mountainous country, road, caravan, their burning crossroads; parched

Hebrew: passer from beyond, an Eberite

Hebrews: descendants of Heber

Herod: son of a hero, heroic

Iconium: coming

Isaac: laughter, he shall laugh, mockery

Isaiah: the salvation of the Lord

Israel: who prevails with God, prince of God

Italy: abounding with calves or heifers

Jacob: that supplants, undermines, heel-catcher

James: that supplants, undermines, heel-catcher, he whom God protects

Jason: he that cures

Jerusalem: vision of peace, foundation of peace, restoring or teaching of peace

Jesse: gift, oblation, one who is, possessor, wealthy, Yahweh exists, man, manly, strong

Jesus: Savior, Deliverer, Yahweh is salvation

Jew: the praise of the Lord, confession

Joel: he that wills or commands, Jehovah is God

John: the grace or mercy of the Lord

Joppa: beauty, comeliness

Joseph: increase, addition, may God add

Joshua: a savior, a deliverer

Judas: the praise of the Lord, confession

Julius: downy, soft and tender hair

Jupiter: the father that helpeth

Justus: just or upright

Kish: hard, difficult, straw, for age, bow, power

Lasea: thick, wise

Levite: descendant of Levi, joined to

Libya: the heart of the sea, fat

Lycaonia: she-wolf

Lydda: Lydia, a standing pool

Lydia: Lydia, a standing pool

Lysias: dissolving

Lystra: that dissolves or disperses

Macedonia: burning, adoration

Manaen: a comforter, a leader

Mark: polite, shining

Mary: bitterness, rebellion

Matthew: given, a reward, gift of Jehovah

Matthias: the gift of God

Medes: middle land

Mesopotamia: between two rivers, exalted

Midian: judgment, covering, habit, contention, strife

Mitylene: purity, cleansing, press

Mnason: a diligent seeker, an exhorter

Moses: taken out, drawn forth

Myra: I flow, pour out, weep

Mysia: criminal, abominable

Nazareth: separated, crowned, sanctified, watchtower

Neapolis: the new city

Nicanor: a conqueror, victorious

Niger: black

Pamphylia: a nation made up of every tribe

Paphos: which boils, or is very hot

Parmenas: that abides, or is permanent

Passover: to pass or to spring over, to spare

Patara: trodden under foot

Paul: small, little

Paulus: small, little

Pentecost: fiftieth

Perga: very earthy

Peter: a rock or stone

Pharaoh: that disperses, that spoils, great house, his nakedness

Pharisees: set apart

Philippi: warlike, a lover of horses

Phrygia: dry, barren

Pilate: armed with a dart, cap of freedom

Pisidia: pitch, pitchy

Pontius: marine, belonging to the sea

Priscilla: ancient

Prochorus: he that presides over the choirs

Psalms: songs of praise

Publius: common

Puteoli: sulphurous wells

Rhegium: rupture, fracture

Rhoda: a rose

Rhodes: a rose

Roman: from Rome, strong, powerful

Rome: strength, power

Sadducees: followers of Sadoc, or Zadok, righteous

Salamis: shaken, test, beaten

Samaria: watch-mountain

Samaritans: inhabitants of Samaria

Samos: full of gravel

Samuel: heard of God, asked of God

Sapphira: that relates or tells

Satan: contrary, adversary, enemy, accuser, deceiver

Saul: demanded, lent, ditch, death

Sceva: disposed, prepared

Secundus: second

Seleucia: shaken or beaten by the waves

Sergius: net

Sharon: his plain, his song, excellence, beauty, to be smooth

Shechem: part, portion, back early in the morning, shoulder, diligence

Sidon: hunting, fishing, venison

Silas: three, or the third

Simeon: that hears or obeys, that is heard

Simon: that hears, that obeys

Sin: bush, thorn

Sinai: a bush, enmity, thorny

Solomon: peaceable, perfect, one who recompenses

Sopater: Sosipater, who defends the father

Sosthenes: savior, strong, powerful

Stephen: crown, crowned

Syracuse: that draws violently

Syria: Aram, exalted, high tableland

Tabitha: clear-sighted, a roe-deer

Tarsus: winged, feathered

Tertullus: third

Tetrarch: governor of a fourth part

Theophilus: friend of God

Thessalonica: victory against the Thessalians

Theudas: flowing with water

Thomas: a twin

Thyatira: a perfume, sacrifice of labor

Timon: honorable, worthy

Titus: pleasing

Troas: penetrated

Trophimus: well educated, well brought up

Tychicus: casual, by chance

Tyrannus: a prince, one that reigns

Tyre: Tyrus, strength, rock, sharp

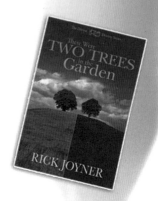
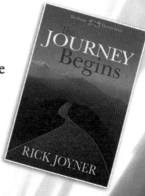

MorningStar PC Study Bible

We believe this is the most powerful, easy to use Bible and Christian research program available, and it would be a value at several times this price. —Rick Joyner

Premium Edition

Our Price $159.00
Retail $199.00 You Save $40.00

Includes all of the books in the Standard Edition PLUS:

- Several additional Bible translations and commentaries
- Over 50 books from church history
- Also includes: *The Final Quest* Series, The *Overcoming* Series and more!

A LA CARTE VALUE OF $2,200

Standard Edition

Our Price $79.00
Retail $99.00 You Save $20.00

Includes:

- Multiple Bible Translations
- Complete Bible Commentary
- Bible History Collection
- Maps, Photos, & Much More
- PLUS: Nine of MorningStar's Books

A LA CARTE VALUE OF $860